THE
FORGOTTEN
FRONTIER

COMMERCIAL STREET, ATCHISON, KANSAS.—Sketched by William M. Merrick.—[See Page 477.]

THE FORGOTTEN FRONTIER

URBAN PLANNING IN THE AMERICAN WEST BEFORE 1890

JOHN W. REPS

UNIVERSITY OF MISSOURI PRESS

COLUMBIA & LONDON, 1981

Copyright © 1981 by
The Curators of the University of Missouri
Library of Congress Catalog Card Number 81-10322
Printed and bound in the United States of America
University of Missouri Press, Columbia, Missouri 65211

Library of Congress Cataloging in Publication Data

Reps, John William.
      The forgotten frontier.

      Bibliography: p. 148
      Includes index.
      1. City planning—West (U.S.)—History—19th
century.   2. Urbanization—West (U.S.)—History—
19th century.
HT123.R44   1981   307.7'6'0978   81-10322
ISBN 0-8262-0351-5
ISBN 0-8262-0352-3 (pbk.)   AACR2

TO THE MEMORY OF
MITCHELL A. WILDER

RAILROAD BUILDING ON THE GREAT PLAINS.—Drawn by A. R. Waud.—[See Page 579.]

PREFACE

This book is based on two other treatments of the role of urbanization and town planning in the settlement of the West. The more extended of the two is my *Cities in the American West: A History of Frontier Urban Planning*, published in 1979 by Princeton University Press.

The research and writing of that volume occupied more than a decade, and its completion was possible only through the generous help of the Amon Carter Museum of Western Art in Fort Worth, Texas. Throughout that period I enjoyed the constant encouragement and counsel of its late director, Mitchell A. Wilder. He originally approached me with a much more modest study in mind, but as the scope of my inquiry broadened, and the manuscript assumed unforeseen dimensions, he tolerantly continued his support and was patient and gracious with his advice.

Mitchell Wilder died while the resulting book was in press. It is to his memory that the present work is dedicated in gratitude for his help. I am also indebted to his associate, Ronnie C. Tyler, Director of Publications of the Amon Carter Museum; and to Professor Ian Stewart, now a Cornell colleague, who for two years during the early period of the project was my research assistant. Countless other persons extended their help, both at Cornell and in scores of libraries, museums, and public offices throughout the West.

The second work upon which this book is based developed from an invitation from its sponsors to submit a paper for the first international conference on the history of planning, held in London in September 1977. I elected to prepare an extended summary of *Cities of the American West*, then still in the process of publication.

This present book is an elaboration of that unpublished conference paper; many of the early footnotes now appear in the bibliographical note, references to more recent scholarship have been added, and the presentation has been reorganized throughout. To the principal organizers of that stimulating and productive London conference—Professor Gordon E. Cherry and Mr. Anthony Sutcliffe—I wish to express my thanks for a challenging assignment and to explain, with the appearance of this book, why I chose to withhold my paper, in its original abbreviated form, from the published proceedings of that meeting.

Because city planning histories of the West—even of individual towns and cities—are so few in number, I have not included a formal bibliography. Instead, the reader will find unusually copious footnotes that serve as a more useful guide to source material and to suggest avenues for further research and study. The illustrations are mainly selected from the more than five hundred appearing in the parent volume, although a few new ones have been added.

J.W.R.
Ithaca, N.Y.
June 1981

CONTENTS

THE FORGOTTEN FRONTIER

URBAN PLANNING IN THE AMERICAN WEST BEFORE 1890

THE TURNER HYPOTHESIS AND THE AMERICAN WESTERN FRONTIER

In 1825 only a handful of tiny and widely separated urban settlements existed in the American West. During the next sixty-five years, a restless and land-hungry people swept across the Western half of the continent, planning and building thousands of new communities in an unprecedented manner. Most historians of the West have overlooked the magnitude and significance of this achievement. Focusing their attention mainly on rural settlement of the frontier, they have minimized the roles towns played in the process of Western expansion, failing to note that the creation of new towns preceded or occurred simultaneously with the opening of lands for farming and ranching.

Largely responsible for this oversight was the frontier hypothesis expounded by Frederick Jackson Turner and the preoccupation of American historians with its implications. Turner first presented his views on the frontier in a paper delivered before a meeting of the American Historical Association at Chicago in 1893. He maintained that it was the constant availability of open land for Western expansion that had molded the American character, which he described as "that coarseness and strength combined with acuteness and inquisitiveness; that practical, inventive turn of mind, quick to find expedients; that masterful grasp of material things, lacking in the artistic but powerful to effect great ends; that restless, nervous energy; that dominant individualism, working for good and for evil, and withal that buoyancy and exuberance which comes with freedom."[1]

Turner introduced his paper with a quotation from the superintendent of the census: "Up to and including 1880 the country had a frontier of settlement, but at present the unsettled area has been so broken into by isolated bodies of settlement that there can hardly be said to be a frontier line." This short statement, Turner asserted, marked "the closing of a great historic movement," an event that he suggested would have profound consequences for the future of American society. Indeed, since according to his theory the democratic nature of American institutions had its origin in the frontier experience, the "closing" of the frontier might well bring undesirable changes in the years ahead.

1. This and other quotations from Frederick Jackson Turner, "The Significance of the Frontier in American History," are from the original version in the *Annual Report of the American Historical Association* (Washington, D.C., 1894). For comments on this and other writings by Turner, for the treatment of Western urbanization by American historians and geographers, and for suggestions for further research, see the Bibliographical Note to this work.

In his paper Turner also quoted from a guide to the West published in 1837. Its author described how unsettled land was first occupied by the trapper and hunter, then by the farmer, and only at a much later stage by "men of capital and enterprise" who enlarged the "small village" of the previous occupants into "a spacious town or city" with "substantial edifices of brick . . . , colleges and churches."[2] This concept of a fixed sequence of exploration—hunting and trapping, the clearing of land for farming, the formation of small hamlets and village centers, and, finally, the gradual development of cities— provided the basis for a more detailed statement in a widely used text on the westward movement by Ray Allen Billington.

According to Billington, "As the westward movement gained momentum, a standardized zonal pattern developed which, although varying slightly with time and place, remained largely consistent until the continent was occupied." Billington distinguished six such "zones," beginning with the "domain of the fur traders," followed by those of the "cattlemen," the miners, "the pioneer farmers," the "equipped farmers," and, only then, "the final frontier zone" of urbanization.

Billington described how towns came into existence during this concluding phase of frontier development: "The specialists drawn to the West by the magnet of opportunity—millers, merchants, grain dealers, slaughterers, distillers, speculators, schoolmasters, dancing teachers, lawyers, and editors— chose their homesites at strategically located points in the center of agricultural communities, usually selecting a crossroads, a point at the head of navigation on some stream, or an advantageous spot on a canal or railroad. As more and more concentrated there, a hamlet, then a village, then a town, gradually took shape."[3]

While this notion of a "standardized zonal pattern" may have had some limited validity in characterizing the settlement of America east of Turner's native Wisconsin, it was almost entirely erroneous for the region beyond the 95th meridian. The simple truth is that in every section of the West, towns were in the vanguard of settlement. They were established as planned communities from the beginning, with designs that provided a framework for future growth. They led the way and shaped the structure of society rather than merely following and responding to the needs of an agrarian population for

2. In his original paper Turner identified this as *Peck's New Guide to the West*. In a revised version with additional material and notes, he listed elsewhere John M. Peck, *A New Guide to the West* (Cincinnati, 1848). In a later essay, published, with others, in *The Frontier in American History* (New York, 1920), Turner repeated this theme: "Stand at Cumberland Gap and watch the procession of civilization, marching single file—the buffalo, following the trail to the salt springs, the Indian, the fur-trader and hunter, the cattle-raiser, the pioneer farmer—and the frontier has passed by. Stand at South Pass in the Rockies a century later and see the same procession with wider intervals between" (p. 12).

3. Ray Allen Billington, *Westward Expansion: A History of the American Frontier* (New York, 1949), pp. 3–6.

markets and points of distribution. They served as the centers of trade and transportation, mining and manufacturing, art and architecture, printing and publishing, religion, recreation, education, administration, banking, and politics. In virtually every aspect of life, urban residents, not farmers and ranchers, dominated Western culture.

Western towns, moreover, differed little from their Eastern counterparts. Most were founded by promoters and settled by migrants from the East who brought with them older urban values, expectations, and institutions. Western towns quickly took on the appearance and character of those in other regions of the nation. The editor of a Portland, Oregon, journal, writing in 1886, suggested that if an Eastern city resident were suddenly "set . . . down on the streets of Portland . . . he would observe little difference between his new surroundings and those he beheld but a moment before in his native city." He would find "the rows of substantial brick blocks . . . , the well-paved and graded streets, the lines of street railway, the mass of telegraph and telephone wires, the numerous electric lights and street lamps, the fire-plugs and water hydrants, the beautiful private residences surrounded by lawns and shade trees suggesting years of careful culture, the long lines of wharves and warehouses on the river front, and the innumerable other features common to every prosperous Eastern city and commercial port."[4]

Although Portland was older than most Western urban communities, its achievements were not untypical. A detailed report on urban services, which appeared as part of the census of 1880, revealed that in this respect many Western communities compared favorably with cities in the South and East. In varying degrees, Western cities lighted streets, supplied water and gas, regulated the disposal of sewage, collected garbage, constructed and maintained streets and sidewalks, operated markets, fought crime, furnished mass transportation, cared for the sick, buried the dead, extinguished fires, controlled nuisances, educated their youth, and provided recreational facilities.[5]

By focusing on the frontier as an agricultural phenomenon, the Turnerians have also failed to emphasize sufficiently that settlers moved westward for a variety of purposes in addition to their quest for cheap and productive farms and ranches. Many came primarily to found towns and to speculate in urban land. Others built the railroads and the communities along the railroads that

4. Blake McKelvey, in his *The Urbanization of America, 1860–1915* (New Brunswick, N.J., 1963), p. 34, calls attention to the influence of Eastern capital and customs in founding and settling towns in the West. The passage describing Portland is from "Portland," *The West Shore* (January 1886): 11. Billington in his *Westward Expansion* and elsewhere in his writings states the opposite case, arguing that Western towns differed sharply from Eastern cities in their appearance, social patterns, political activities, economic roles, and other elements.

5. Lawrence H. Larsen and Robert L. Branyan, "The Development of an Urban Civilization on the Frontier of the American West," *Societas—A Review of Social History* 1 (Winter 1971): 33–50.

were needed to make them profitable. Tens of thousands found their way to the West to mine the rich veins of gold, silver, lead, and copper, lured by expectations of easy wealth and instant prosperity.

For the Mormons, the West beckoned as a sanctuary from religious intolerance and persecution. Much earlier, Jesuits and Franciscans saw in the West an opportunity to bring Christianity to the Indians and to transform them from their pastoral or nomadic ways to urban dwellers. The West also served as a great geopolitical arena where American, English, and Spanish military bases and civil settlements were deployed in an effort to occupy and control ill-defined and often conflicting domains.

Indeed, the American West attracted settlers for the same reasons, goals, and motives that have driven or pulled men and women from one location to another throughout history. Not least of these was the spirit of pure adventure, the desire to be where something new was happening and where, perhaps, ability and energy alone could create the status that elsewhere depended on family background, inherited wealth, or the advantages of education.

The forces stimulating Western settlement were thus much more varied than Turner realized or made explicit. He did, however, call attention to one aspect of Western growth bearing on this point. In tracing how the frontier line moved from the Atlantic seaboard to the Midwest, he noted that the "gold discoveries had sent a sudden tide of adventurous miners" to California where they, along with even earlier pioneers in Oregon and Utah, created a pattern of several detached frontiers.

It was the movement of these detached frontiers toward one another that, by 1890, created a more or less continuous zone of settlement. Turner understood that this movement had been hastened by the construction of transcontinental rail lines, the completion of which sent "an increasing tide of immigrants into the far West." Although much land remained to be occupied, the frontier as an evermoving line delimiting areas devoted to farming from those yet unsettled was, by 1890, indeed a thing of the past.

At least of equal importance was that the frontier of the *urban* West had also undergone drastic alteration. By 1890 the basic matrix of towns and cities that would shape community growth in the years to follow had already been cast. Of the thirty-one Western urbanized areas with a 1970 population of two hun-

6. See the Appendix for city population in 1890 and urban area population in 1970 arranged in rank order for both dates.

dred thousand or more, all but one had been founded by 1890. In that year there were twenty cities in the West with populations exceeding twenty thousand. Of these, only four did not rank among the thirty-one largest of 1970. (For specific population data, see the Appendix.)[6]

For the historian of city planning, the frontier period ended in another way as well. In most cases the original pattern of urban land division provided ample room for growth, with streets, blocks, lots, civic spaces, and public building sites generously laid out to accommodate development well beyond the first increment of building. Even in cases where the first design proved inadequate in size, its influence on the subsequent growth and character of the expanding city proved enormous.

Thus, nearly every Western town and city began as a planned settlement whose physical forms were determined in advance by individuals, corporations, colonization societies, religious groups, or public officials. Nothing could be further from the truth than the notion that Western towns originated as spontaneous crossroads hamlets that grew slowly, incrementally, and randomly, without guidance or direction. The West was a region of planned cities.

PLANNED TOWNS OF THE HISPANIC WEST

In his observations on detached areas of settlement, Turner ignored a far older frontier where the first Western towns were planned. This frontier stretched across the northern borderlands of the vast Spanish colonial empire from Texas, through New Mexico and Arizona, and up the California coast. From the first decade of the seventeenth century until almost the middle of the nineteenth century, the Spanish and Mexican governments pursued a policy of town development in this region. Their efforts laid the foundations for some of the largest cities in the region—Los Angeles, San Francisco, San José, San Diego, Albuquerque, Tucson, and San Antonio—and for such smaller but historically important communities as Sonoma, Monterey, Santa Fe, and Laredo.[7]

7. Not included in this list is El Paso, Texas, where the population of the urbanized area in 1970 was 337,471. While its location was the site of two or three small Spanish missions, the main colonial settlement was on the Mexican side of the Rio Grande in what is now Ciudad Juárez.

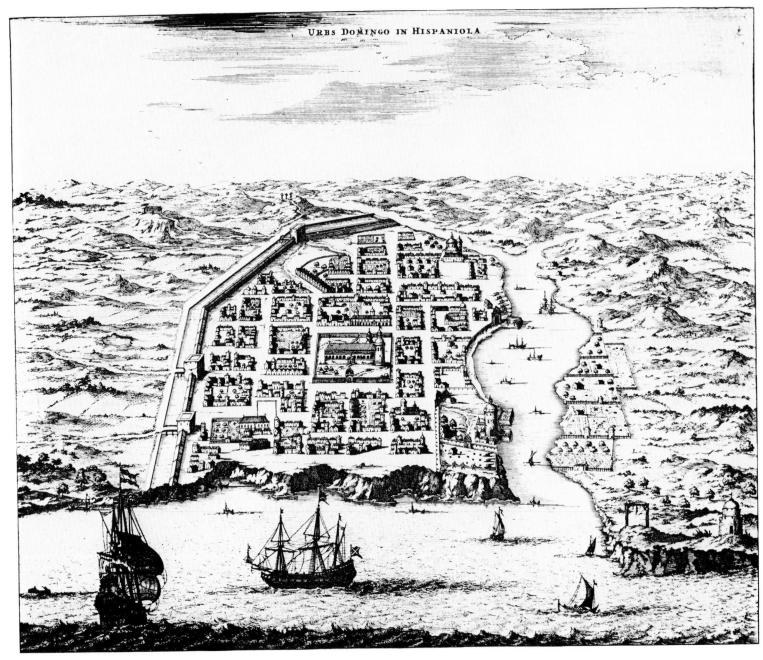

URBS DOMINGO IN HISPANIOLA

Figure 1. Santo Domingo, Dominican Republic, based on a view first published in 1588

8. A small woodcut view of La Navidad appeared in an illustrated edition of a letter from Columbus to Gabriel Sánchez published in Basel in 1493. A reproduction can be found in *The Journal of Christopher Columbus*, trans. Cecil Jane (New York, 1960), p. 127.

9. The earliest printed depiction of Santo Domingo showing the details of its plan appeared in *Expeditio Francisci Draki Equitis Angli in Indias Occidentalis* (Leiden, 1588). This print was used as the basis for the illustration published in Theodor de Bry, *Americae achter Theil . . . , Additamentum* (Frankfort, 1600). That these plan-views are reasonably faithful representations of Santo Domingo as it was originally planned is suggested by a resident's description of the city in 1526. See Gonzalo Fernandez de Oviedo, *Natural History of the West Indies* (Toledo, 1526), trans. and ed. Sterling A. Stoudemire (Chapel Hill, N.C., 1959), pp. 11–13.

10. The first English translation of the town planning provisions of the Laws of the Indies is Zelia Nuttall, "Royal Ordinances Concerning the Laying Out of New Towns," *Hispanic American Historical Review* 5 (1922): 249–54. A new translation, with additional provisions of the laws relevant to urban development and with explanatory notes and commentary, can be found in Axel I. Mundigo and Dora P. Crouch, "The City Planning Ordinances of the Laws of the Indies Revisited, Part I: Their Philosophy and Implications," *Town Planning Review* 48 (July 1977): 247–68. See also Dora P. Crouch and Axel I. Mundigo, "The City Planning Ordinances of the Laws of the Indies Revisited, Part II: Three American Cities," *Town Planning Review* 48 (October 1977): 397–418. Oakah L. Jones, Jr., *Los Paisanos: Spanish Settlers on the Northern Frontier of New Spain* (Norman, Okla., 1979), traces how laws influenced urban settlement during the colonial period in northern Mexico and in the adjoining borderlands from Texas to California.

The planning of these cities continued the tradition begun in December 1492 when Columbus founded Spain's first outpost in the New World. This was La Navidad, built in part from the timbers of the wrecked *Santa Maria* on the northern coast of the island of Hispañiola.[8] It did not survive, nor did Isabela, the earliest true town planned by Europeans in the Western Hemisphere, which was built on a location selected by Columbus in 1493, a few miles to the east of La Navidad. The oldest surviving town of Hispanic origins is Santo Domingo, surveyed on its present site in 1502 after a tropical storm destroyed an earlier community nearby.[9]

Santo Domingo's plan introduced to the Americas the pattern of grid streets and plazas that was to govern Spanish colonial urban design for more than four hundred years (Figure 1). The town planning experience at Santo Domingo was systematically reported to officials in Spain, and as later expeditions left to settle other parts of the New World, their leaders received directions governing the location and planning of towns. These became progressively more detailed, and in 1573 Philip II proclaimed a detailed set of regulations and colonization rules incorporating what had been learned.[10]

These Laws of the Indies were expected to govern the planning of all subsequent settlements in what by then was an extensive colonial empire. This vast overseas domain could not have functioned without an intricate urban network composed of ports, mining towns, military communities, administrative centers, religious complexes, and viceregal and provincial capitals. However, at least in what is now the United States, colonial town planners rarely followed all of the scores of regulations composing the Laws of the Indies.

One provision of the laws, for example, clearly specified that two streets should extend from each corner of the elongated rectangle formed by the main plaza and that wider main thoroughfares should enter the plaza at the midpoints of each side, for a total of twelve streets emanating from the plaza. There appears to be no case in the American West where this regulation was carried out, although the 1781 plan for Los Angeles seems to represent an attempt to comply with this requirement.

Other elements of the laws, however, were generally put into practice: a grid street plan, the creation of a main plaza and subsidiary open spaces, the location of the main buildings facing the plaza, the reservation of common land around the town, a systematic method of allotting land to the settlers, and other matters. This first American urban planning legislation, therefore, substantially influenced the design of communities in a large portion of the American West.

This era of Spanish town planning began with the founding of Santa Fe by Don Pedro de Peralta in 1609. His new town provided an administrative, religious, and military center for New Mexico, a province lying on the northern edge of the Spanish colonial domain. No early surveys of Santa Fe are known to exist; for information about its original plan we must rely on a drawing made more than a century and a half after the town came into being. This oldest surviving graphic record of Santa Fe was the work of Joseph de Urrutia in 1766, one of the many detailed manuscript surveys by him of military and civil settlements in northern Mexico and what is now Texas, New Mexico, and Arizona.[11]

Urrutia's drawing shows a long, rectangular plaza. The church occupies a site near the plaza's southeastern corner, the governor's residence is along the western end of the north side, and facing it is the military chapel on the south side of the plaza (Figure 2). Indications of streets are sketchy, but from the alignment of the other buildings in the town it appears that they were straight and intersected at right angles.

More information exists about the planning of San Antonio, founded as the first civil settlement of Spanish Texas in 1731. Earlier Spanish efforts had been confined to the establishment of a series of missions and military posts in the southern and eastern parts of the province, including the mission of San Antonio de Valero (now the Alamo) and a presidio, or fort, nearby on the opposite side of the San Antonio River.

To consolidate the settlement of this portion of Texas and to help solve the problem of providing food to the presidio, the viceroy resolved to create a town at this location. Officials in Spain approved his recommendation and arranged for a group of Canary Islanders to be transported to Mexico and then taken by land to the selected spot. They brought with them detailed instructions on how to proceed and a drawing prepared in 1730 showing how the town was to be planned (Figure 3).

Although the arrangement of the streets around the plaza departed somewhat from the Laws of the Indies pattern, the plan of San Antonio de Bejar was otherwise in general conformity with their specifications. This design

11. The Urrutia drawings can be found in the Manuscripts Room of The British Library in London. Those of Santa Fe and San Antonio are reproduced in color in John W. Reps, *Cities of the American West: A History of Frontier Urban Planning* (Princeton, 1979), pls. 3, 4. Others of frontier presidios in Texas and Arizona appear as figs. 3.12, 3.13, and 4.1, on pp. 76, 77, and 88.

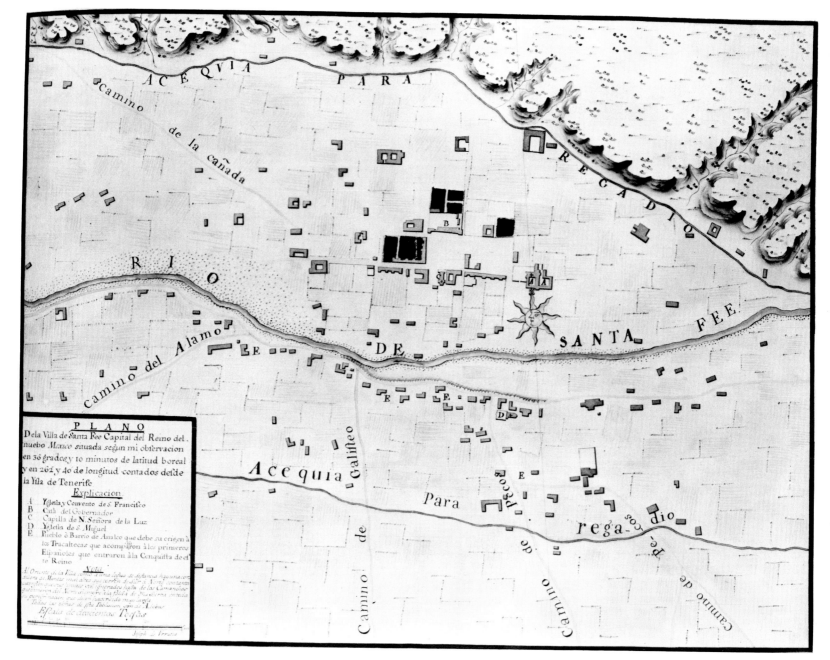

Figure 2. Santa Fe, New Mexico, in 1766

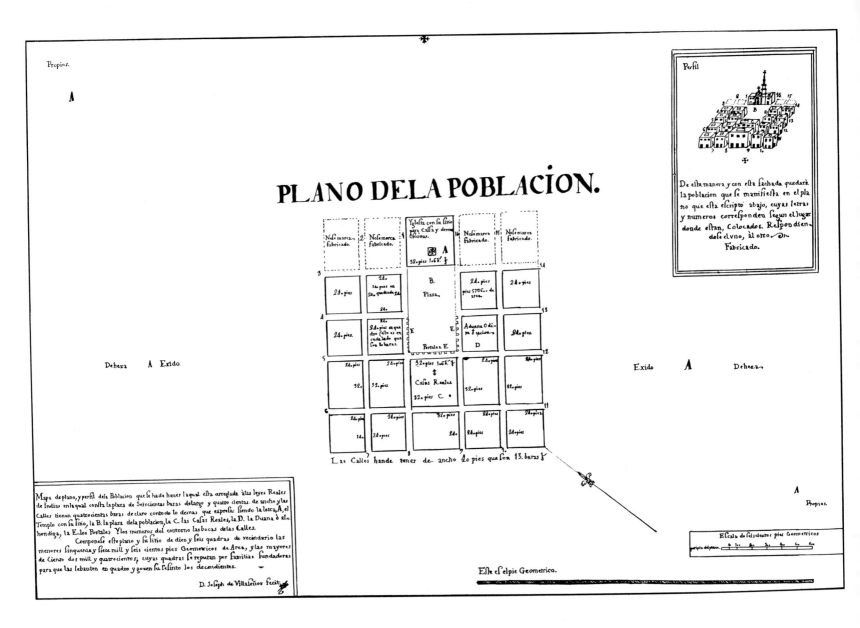

Figure 3. Plan for San Antonio, Texas, in 1730

illustrates one additional requirement of the laws: the orientation of the grid street system so that the four corners of the plaza and of the blocks faced directly north, south, east, and west. This was intended to prevent the winds—supposed to come always from the cardinal points of the compass—from blowing unchecked down the town's streets.

When the exact site described in the instructions, "a gunshot's distance to the western side of the presidio," proved unsatisfactory, the commanding officer decided to place the town immediately adjacent to the military post. In order to do this, he altered the prescribed plan by reducing the size of the plaza and by rotating the street grid almost forty-five degrees.[12]

In Urrutia's drawing of San Antonio in 1767 one can see the town's plaza separated by the church from the military plaza (Figure 4). A few streets, generally rectangular in alignment, can just be discerned, but it is obvious that a description of the community a decade later was not exaggerated: "The town consists of fifty-nine houses of stone and mud and seventy-nine of wood, but all poorly built, without any preconceived plan, so that the whole resembles more a poor village than a villa, capital of so pleasing a province. . . . The streets are tortuous and are filled with mud the minute it rains."[13]

Dusty or muddy, the streets and plazas of colonial San Antonio provided the basic structure for the town as it slowly grew in population and expanded in size during the next century. Its civil plaza and church served as the focal point for social and religious life and as a place for markets and fiestas. Adobe buildings, mostly one story high, surrounded the plaza, defining its shape and enclosing it in almost exactly the manner that the Spanish officials had envisioned, although it had taken far longer to develop than they had anticipated (Figure 5).

Conditions in the two earliest California towns were equally primitive. Founded by Gov. Felipe de Neve, these towns were similar to San Antonio in that they were expected to help supply the three presidios already established at San Diego, Monterey, and San Francisco. First at San José in 1777, and then at Los Angeles in 1781, Neve attempted to apply the Laws of the Indies in his town designs.[14]

The first known survey of Los Angeles (redrawn for easier understanding) shows only the plaza, the sites facing it, and the openings between them for the streets that Neve surveyed (Figure 6). On two sides and on part of a third,

12. Lota M. Spell, "The Grant and First Survey of the City of San Antonio," *Southwestern Historical Review* 66 (July 1962): 73–89.

13. Juan Agustín Morfi, *History of Texas, 1673–1779*, trans. and ed. Carlos Eduardo Castañeda (Albuquerque, N.M., 1935), 1: 92.

14. For the founding of San José, see Frederick Hall, *The History of San José and Surroundings* (San Francisco, 1871); and Oscar Osburn Winther, "The Story of San José, 1777–1869, Chapter I: The Spanish Period," *California Historical Society Quarterly* 14 (March 1935): 3–27.

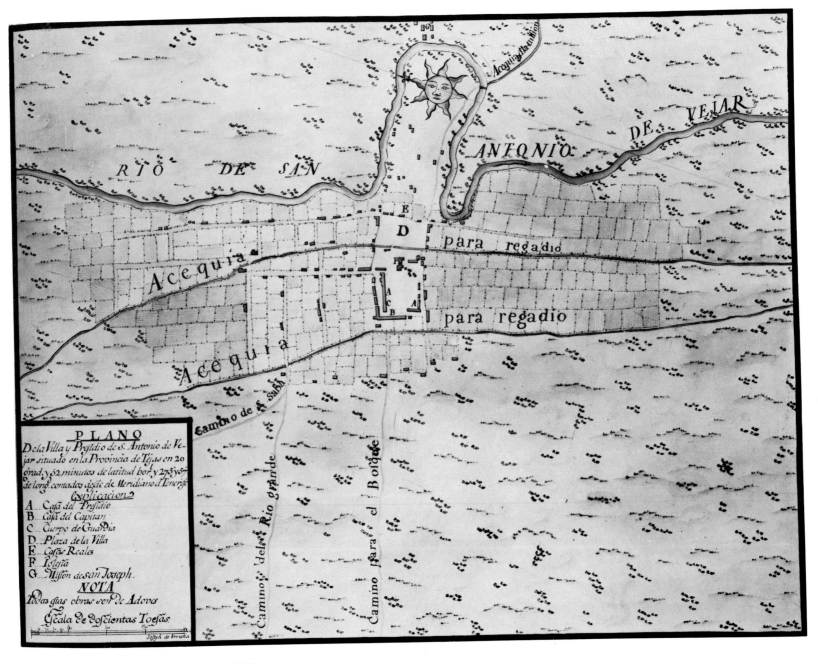

Figure 4. San Antonio, Texas, in 1767

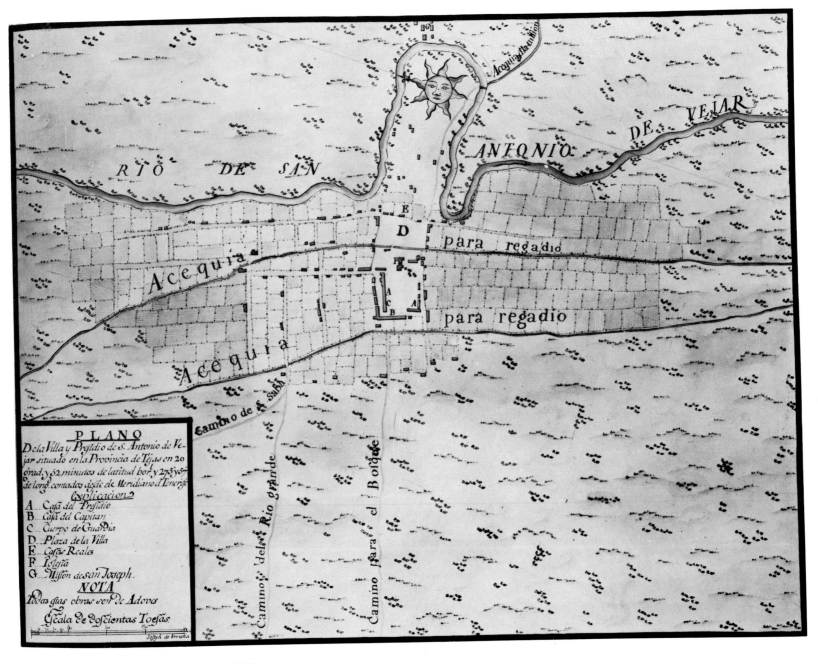 contains labels within the map:

RIO DE SAN ANTONIO DE VEIAR

Acequia para Mission

Acequia

Acequia

para regadio

para regadio

Camino de S. Saba

Camino del Rio grande

Camino para el Bosque

PLANO

De la Villa y Presidio de S. Antonio de Ve-
jar situado en la Provincia de Tejas en 29
grad. y 32 minutos de latitud bor. y 275 y 57
de long. contados desde de Meridiano d Tenerife

Esplicacion

A ... Casa del Presidio
B ... Casa del Capitan
C ... Cuerpo de Guardia
D ... Plaza de la Villa
E ... Casas Reales
F ... Iglesia
G ... Mission de san Joseph.

NOTA

Todas estas obras son de Adoves

Escala de doscientas Toesas

Joseph de Urrutia

12 · The Forgotten Frontier

Figure 5. West side of the main plaza in San Antonio, Texas, in 1849

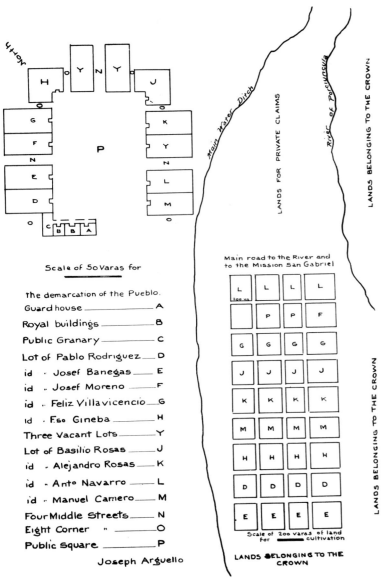

NORTH

Scale of 50 Varas for

the demarcation of the Pueblo.
Guard house ———————— A
Royal buildings ——————— B
Public Granary ——————— C
Lot of Pablo Rodriguez —— D
id • Josef Banegas ———— E
id • Josef Moreno ———— F
id • Feliz Villavicencio — G
id • Fso Gineba ————— H
Three Vacant Lots ———— Y
Lot of Basilio Rosas ——— J
id • Alejandro Rosas —— K
id • Anto Navarro ———— L
id • Manuel Camero ——— M
Four Middle Streets —— N
Eight Corner " ———— O
Public square ————— P

Joseph Arguello

Certificate of José Fᶜᵒ de Ortega Lieut. & Commandante of the Company. annexed. Company consisted of 12 men as per his review had Jan. 3rd 1782.

Main Water Ditch

LANDS FOR PRIVATE CLAIMS

River of Porcivnasia

LANDS BELONGING TO THE CROWN

Main road to the River and to the Mission San Gabriel

LANDS BELONGING TO THE CROWN

Scale of 200 varas of land for cultivation

LANDS BELONGING TO THE CROWN

Figure 6. Plan of the pueblo of Los Angeles, California, as redrawn from the manuscript survey of 1781

one can see that two streets enter the plaza at each corner and that one enters at the midpoint of each side as called for by the laws. The orientation also fulfilled the peculiar requirement that the corners of the plaza face the cardinal points of the compass. This drawing also indicates, at a much smaller scale, the rectangular farm tracts laid out near the nucleated settlement.[15]

The appearance of Los Angeles during the Spanish and Mexican periods is not recorded in any known drawings or paintings, but by the end of the eighteenth century it must have looked much like American soldiers found it during the Mexican War. Then and for several years thereafter it was little more than a village, dominated visually by the church on one side of the plaza (Figure 7). Leading outward were a few short streets lined by adobe buildings, while beyond lay the farms and ranches of the inhabitants.

A few other Hispanic colonial towns in New Mexico and California were planned in similar fashion, although no two designs were exactly alike. These include Albuquerque, founded in 1706, and the abortive community of Branciforte (now Santa Cruz), California, founded in 1796. Largest in size, although not in population, was Sonoma, planned in 1835 under Mexican rule by Gen. Mariano G. Vallejo (Figure 8). Although Vallejo reported to the Mexican governor that he "traced the streets and divided the houselots as prescribed by the law," Sonoma's design did not, in fact, conform precisely to the Laws of the Indies, if these were the regulations to which he referred.[16]

Other California municipalities came into existence during the Mexican period when groups of settlers near the presidios sought official recognition for town-sized settlements that remained under military jurisdiction. Monterey apparently achieved municipal status sometime in the 1820s. The earliest view of the town, drawn in 1842, suggests that its officials attempted to regulate streets and property lines (Figure 9). A few years before, however, Richard Henry Dana noted that while Monterey made "a very pretty appearance," its hundred or so houses were "dotted about, here and there, irregularly," and he recorded that he could see "no streets nor fences . . . so that the houses are placed at random upon the green."[17]

Residents of San Diego received pueblo rights in 1834 in recognition of their settlement clustered on level ground at the foot of the hill where the presidio stood. Several early views show their buildings arranged around a plaza

15. Conditions in California leading to the founding of San José and Los Angeles and Neve's role in their creation are described in Edwin A. Beilharz, *Felipe de Neve: First Governor of California* (San Francisco, 1971).

16. Mariano G. Vallejo, *Recuerdos historicos y personales tocante a la Alta California*, MS, Bancroft Library, University of California, Berkeley, 1875, 3: 19. For Sonoma's founding, see Lawrence Kinnaird, *History of the Greater San Francisco Bay Region* (New York, 1966), 1: 286–88, 434. Branciforte's history can be traced in Lesley Byrd Simpson, *An Early Ghost Town of California, Branciforte* (San Francisco, 1935). Little seems to be known about the plan of Albuquerque, but the records of its origins are summarized in Lansing B. Bloom, "Albuquerque and Galisteo: Certificate of Their Founding," *New Mexico Historical Review* 10 (January 1935): 48–51.

17. Richard Henry Dana, *Two Years Before the Mast* (1840; Reprint, New York, 1936), p. 73.

Figure 7. Los Angeles, California, in 1853

Figure 8. Sonoma, California, in 1850

HARBOUR and CITY of MONTEREY, California 1842.

Figure 9. Monterey, California, in 1842

18. What is now known as "Old Town" San Diego began as early as 1823. A French visitor a few years later noted that below the presidio "on a sandy plain, are scattered thirty to forty houses of poor appearance, and some badly cultivated gardens." A. Duhaut-Cilly, "Duhaut-Cilly's Account of California in the Years 1827–28," trans. Charles Franklin Carter, *California Historical Society Quarterly* 8 (September 1929): 219. See also William Heath Davis, *Seventy-Five Years in California* (San Francisco, 1929), p. 258, where the author stated that in 1831 "what is now called Old Town was at that date laid out, but it was not built for some time thereafter." Development of San Diego is traced in a series of volumes by Richard F. Pourade, *The History of San Diego* (San Diego, 1960–1965), of which 3: 14–15 has some material on Old Town.

19. For the early years of Yerba Buena, see John W. Dwinelle, *Colonial History of San Francisco* (San Francisco, 1866); Neal Harlow, "The Maps of San Francisco Bay and the town of Yerba Buena to 100 Years Ago," *Pacific Historical Review* 16 (November 1947): 365–78; Zoeth S. Eldredge, *The Beginnings of San Francisco* (San Francisco, 1912); and Gunther Barth, *Instant Cities: Urbanization and the Rise of San Francisco and Denver* (New York, 1975). Barth's study is broader than the title indicates and contains much useful information on such places as Champoeg, Salt Lake City, Santa Fe, Monterey, and Cheyenne, in addition to the two cities on which his work concentrates.

20. For secularization of the California missions, see Irving Berdine Richman, *California under Spain and Mexico, 1535–1847* (Boston, 1911), pp. 228–64, 282–85. The unhappy results are also traced in Daniel Garr, "Planning, Politics and Plunder: The Missions and Indian Pueblos of Hispanic California," *Southern California Quarterly* 54 (Winter 1972): 291–312.

and along what appear to be straight streets (Figure 10). Probably the new municipal council had ordered some kind of plan to be surveyed so that the community could grow with at least a minimum of order and direction.[18]

More is known of the planned beginnings of San Francisco. It occupied a steep slope above Yerba Buena cove inside the Golden Gate and some distance from the presidio, which in 1834 was converted to a municipality and whose lands included all of the upper part of the peninsula between San Francisco Bay and the Pacific Ocean. A year later William Richardson, an English sailor who maintained a hide and tallow warehouse at the spot, arranged with Governor Figueroa to survey a single street as the beginning of a trading town (Figure 11). A month later a second street, intersecting the first at an acute angle, was added.

In 1839 a new governor commissioned the Swiss sailor, tavern keeper, and surveyor, Jean Jacques Vioget, to enlarge the nascent village and to provide a more orderly design (Figure 12). Vioget's plan incorporated the two earlier streets and added a little grid below them with intersections that strangely missed being right angles by two and a half degrees. He reserved a portion of one block near the center of the expanded community as a public square; later, when enlarged, this became the modern Portsmouth Square.[19]

Still other California towns began when the missions were secularized during the Mexican period and some of the former mission property near the churches was laid out in streets, blocks, and lots. While the Indian neophytes received title to building sites, Hispanic and Anglo settlers managed by various means to acquire this property. Thus secularization proved disastrous to the native population. In this manner towns were developed in the vicinity of such missions as San Luis Rey, San Juan Capistrano, San Luis Obispo, and several others, including Santa Clara (Figure 13). A view of the latter town in 1856 probably typifies the appearance of these mission-centered communities after the Franciscans had departed and the mission chapel had assumed new duties as the parish church.[20]

Several small civil settlements, most of them short-lived, were also founded in Texas during the later Spanish period. They included Bucareli in 1774; Nacogdoches, surveyed in 1779 at the site of a deserted mission; Salcedo in 1805 on the east side of the Trinity River across from the abandoned Bucareli; San Marcos in 1807; and Palafox in 1810. Little is known of these communities,

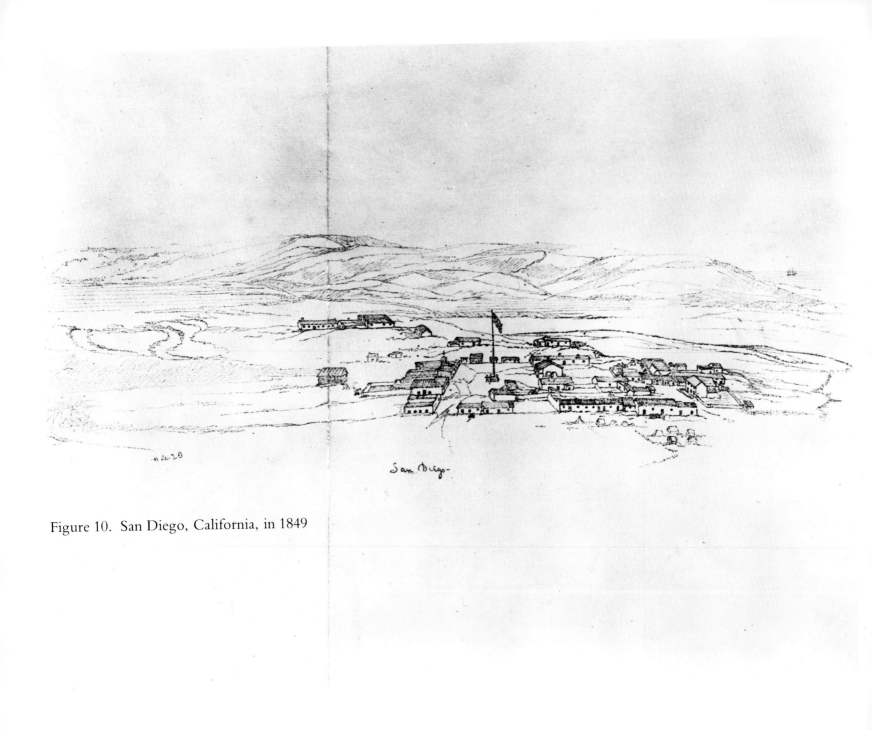

Figure 10. San Diego, California, in 1849

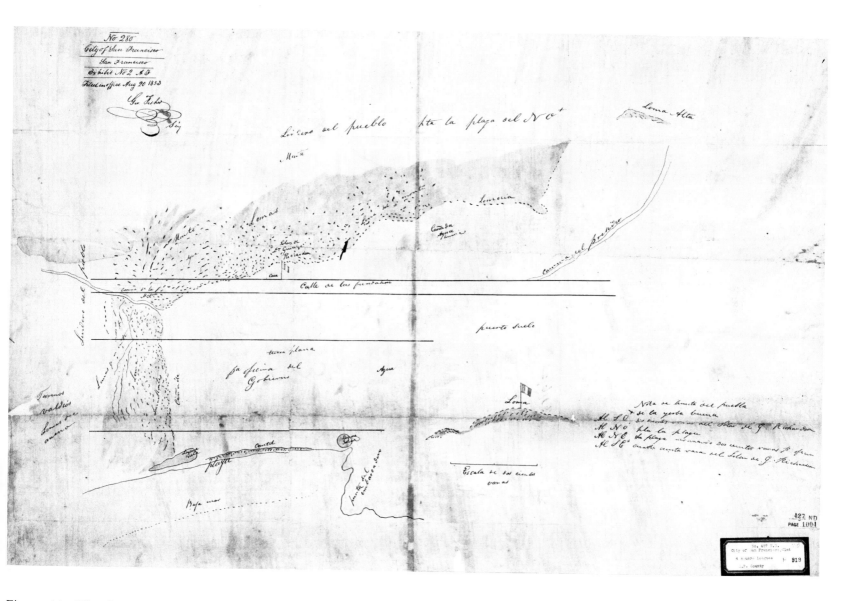

Figure 11. The first street of San Francisco, California, as surveyed in 1835

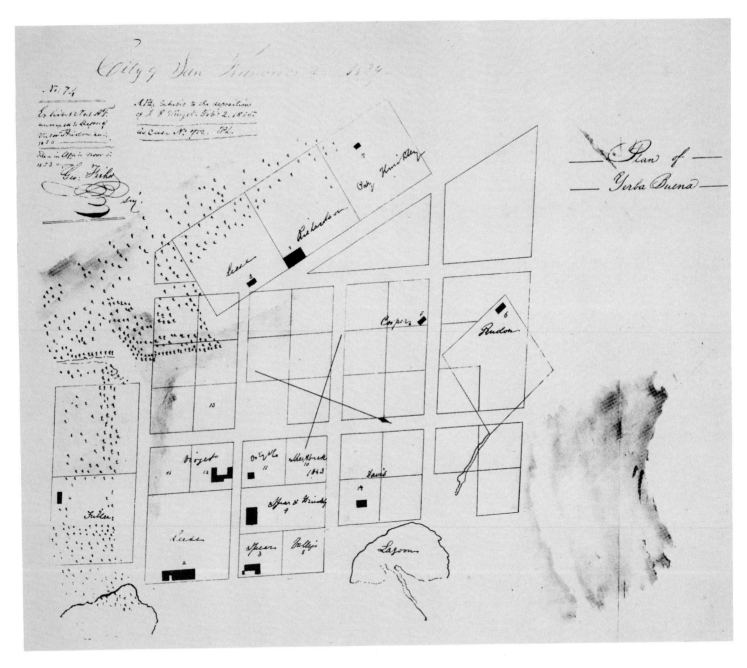

Figure 12. Plan of San Francisco in 1839, drawn by Jean Jacques Vioget

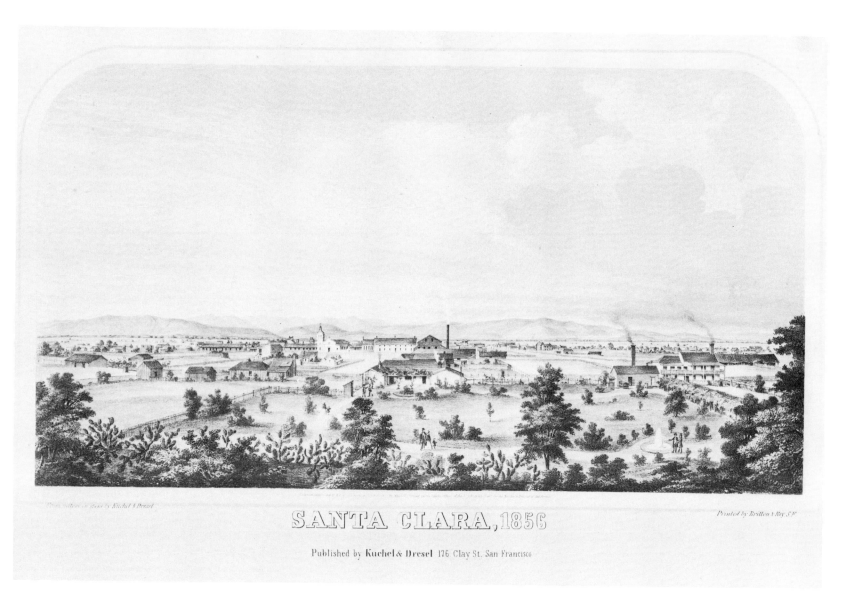

SANTA CLARA, 1856

Published by Kuchel & Dresel 176 Clay St. San Francisco

Figure 13. Santa Clara, California, in 1856

but fragmentary evidence suggests that their founders attempted to follow the Laws of the Indies in their designs.[21]

One important feature of these Spanish and Mexican pueblos or villas should be emphasized. The nucleated settlement was only a part of a larger municipal unit that normally embraced an area of approximately twenty-eight square miles, including farm fields, common pasture and woodland, agricultural tracts leased to produce municipal revenues, and lands reserved for settlers who might come later to join those for whom the towns were founded.

Aside from the initial allocations of town lots and farm fields and lands reserved to the crown, the municipal government, created at the time the town was established, owned all the vast pueblo grant. On the Spanish frontier, therefore, agricultural and urban settlement were simultaneous, and it was a town-centered administrative unit that provided governmental direction of land policy in the years that followed.[22]

URBANIZATION OF EARLY TEXAS

Many elements of Spanish urban planning were also continued in Texas by the Mexican government. To attract settlers to Texas, Mexico in 1825 began a program of large-scale land grants to "empresarios," who received approximately twenty-three thousand acres for every one hundred families they brought with them. The colonization laws specified that each empresario grant was to include a town to be planned under the direction of a public commissioner.

The town development provisions of these statutes closely followed the Laws of the Indies, requiring a plaza, "streets well laid out and straight, running parallel north and south, and east and west," and sites reserved for "a church, curate's dwelling and other ecclesiastical edifices . . . , municipal building . . . , a market square . . . , a jail . . . , school and other buildings for public instruction, and . . . a burial ground." Most of these features appear in Stephen Austin's plan for the first of the empresario towns, San Felipe de Austin, designed in the year prior to the legislation and possibly serving as a model for its provisions (Figure 14).

21. Brief accounts of these Texas towns and an early plan of Palafox can be found in Reps, *Cities of the American West*, pp. 78–84 and fig. 3.15. The plan of Nacogdoches reproduced in fig. 3.14 is of a later period—1846—but it doubtless incorporates at least portions of the original design.

22. The land system and the role of municipalities in the Spanish colonies is dealt with in the following: O. Garfield Jones, "Local Government in the Spanish Colonies as Provided by the Recopilación de Leyes de Los Reynos de Las Indias," *Southwestern Historical Quarterly* 19 (July 1919): 66–69; Herbert I. Priestly, "Spanish Colonial Municipalities," *California Law Review* 7 (1918–1919): 397–416; Marc Simmons, "Spanish Government and Colonial Land Practices," *New Mexico Quarterly* 38 (Spring 1968): 37–43; and Katherine H. White, "Spanish and Mexican Surveying Terms and Systems," *Password* 6 (Winter 1961): 24–27. There is now a fine history of Spanish colonial planning incorporating and expanding on these and other earlier studies: Jones, *Los Paisanos*. Much useful information on the Texas missions, military posts, and civil communities can be found in Carlos E. Castañeda, *Our Catholic Heritage in Texas*, 6 vols. (Austin, 1936–1950). Daniel Garr's unpublished work is noted in Section 10 of the Bibliographical Note. In addition to his article cited in note 20 above, see "A Rare and Desolate Land: Population and Race in Hispanic California," *The Western Historical Quarterly* (April 1975): 133–48; and "A Frontier Agrarian Settlement: San José de Guadelupe, 1777–1850," *San José Studies* 2 (November 1976): 93–105, which includes a reproduction of an early plan of San José previously unknown. Planning in Hispanic New Mexico, Texas, Arizona, and California is treated in three chapters of Reps, *Cities of the American West*, pp. 35–115.

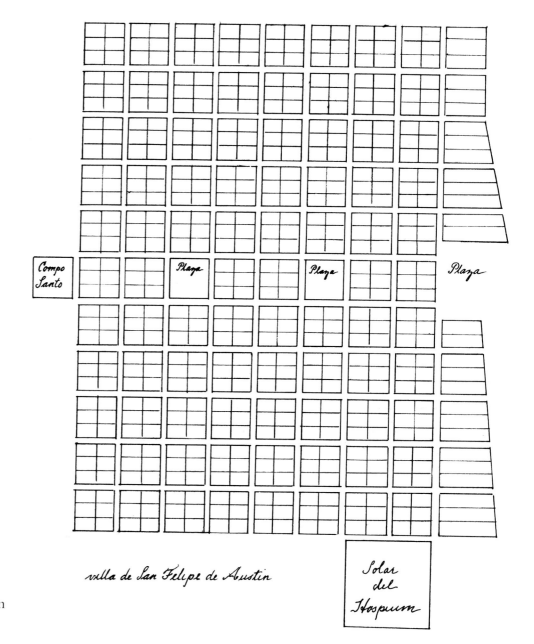

Figure 14. Plan for San Felipe de Austin, redrawn
from a manuscript by Stephen Austin

Under the terms of these laws, each municipality received a generous tract of four square leagues—nearly eighteen thousand acres—corresponding exactly to the size of the Spanish pueblos under the Laws of the Indies. The streets and town lots, of course, occupied only a small portion of this land, much of which was used for farming. Town life and agricultural activities in Mexican Texas thus began simultaneously rather than sequentially, just as settlement had taken place throughout the Southwest under earlier Spanish rule. Much of early nineteenth-century Texas was settled in this pattern. Along with San Felipe, such communities as Victoria, Refugio, San Patricio, Bastrop, Milam, Liberty, Velasco, Matagorda, and Gonzales joined the earlier San Antonio and the few other existing settlements as centers of trade, administration, and social contact.[23]

Certainly the most interesting design of this group was that prepared for Gonzales, which had five open squares arranged in a cruciform pattern at the center of a gridiron consisting of forty-nine square blocks formed by streets fifty-five feet in width (Figure 15). The four main avenues leading to the center were eighty-three feet in width. Sites were provided for the plaza, jail, public buildings, church, parade ground, cemetery, and market. These same sites are still in use today, with only a few modest changes.[24]

Another interesting empresario town was Matagorda, developed by Austin after 1827 when he secured permission to create a port well south of San Felipe. Whether based consciously on the Laws of the Indies or not, the central plaza conformed exactly to their provisions, with a wide street entering it at the middle of each of its four sides and two other thoroughfares leading to it at each of its four corners. A view of Matagorda in 1860 shows that substantial growth took place, partly because of its position as county seat, and partly because its harbor was a popular point of arrival for the European immigrants who were streaming into Texas (Figure 16). Several hurricanes hindered its later development, and a particularly violent storm in 1894 brought its expansion to an end.[25]

Texas independence in 1836 hastened the pace of town planning as thousands of settlers from the United States moved southwestward and were joined by many more from abroad. The new republic, later the state, of Texas seemingly attracted as many urban land speculators as would-be farmers and

23. John Sales and Henry Sales, comps., *Early Laws of Texas* (St. Louis, 1888), 1: 70–74. For colonization under the empresario system, see Leroy P. Graf, "Colonizing Projects in Texas South of the Nueces, 1820–1845," *Southwestern Historical Quarterly* 50 (April 1947): 431–48; Mary Virginia Henderson, "Minor Empresario Contracts for the Colonization of Texas, 1825–1834," *Southwestern Historical Quarterly* 31 (April 1928): 295–324, and 32 (July 1928): 1–29; William H. Oberste, *Texas Irish Empresarios and Their Colonies* (Austin, 1953); Ethel Z. Rather, "De Witt's Colony," *Quarterly of the Texas State Historical Association* 8 (October 1904): 95–191; and Joseph M. White, *A New Collection of Laws . . . of Mexico and Texas* (Philadelphia, 1839), 1: 559–622. The Republic of Texas reinstituted the Mexican empresario system for a brief period. One result was the town of Castroville, at the center of the grant made to Henri Castro of France. Other towns planned on his domain were Qhihi, Vandenburg, and D'Hanis. See Julia Nott Waugh, *Castro-Ville and Henri Castro Empresario* (San Antonio, 1934).

24. A modern aerial view of Gonzales is reproduced in D. W. Meinig's short but perceptive study, *Imperial Texas* (Austin, 1969), fig. 13.

25. A plan of Matagorda in 1835 and of Velasco in 1837 can be found in Reps, *Cities of the American West*, figs. 5.7 and 5.6, pp. 124 and 123.

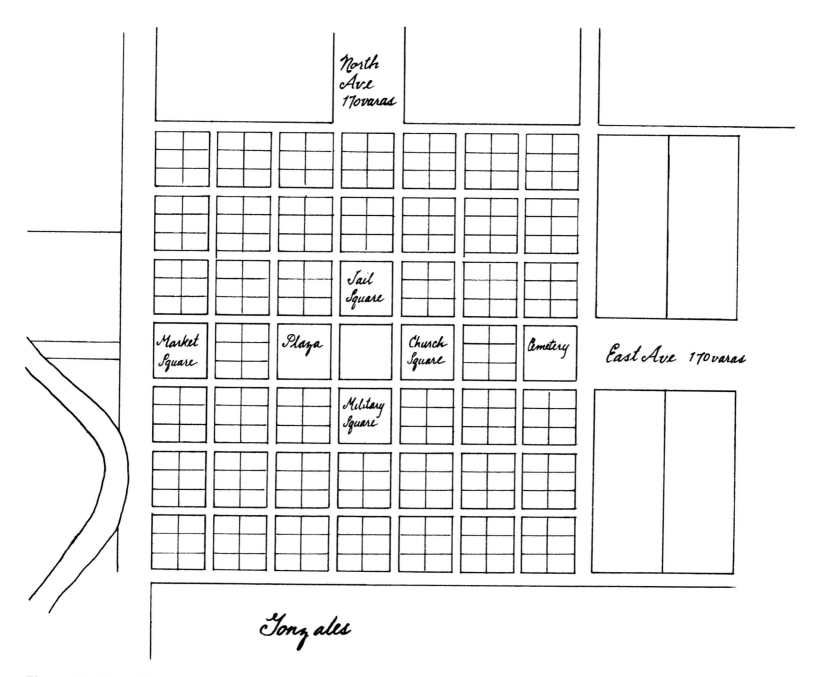

Figure 15. Plan of Gonzales, Texas, in 1836

Figure 16. Matagorda, Texas, in 1860

ranchers. Maps of Texas at the time of statehood in 1845 reveal the existence of scores of thriving new towns—each a planned settlement—where twenty years earlier there had been only San Antonio and perhaps half a dozen other and much smaller communities (Figure 17).

It was during this brief period and in the following decade that most of the major cities in Texas originated. Augustus and John Allen first platted Houston in 1836 and more than doubled its size three years later, indicating that the brothers possessed Texas-size ambitions (Figure 18). In addition to reservations for a school and for churches, they included a full block each for a courthouse and for the capitol of the new republic of Texas. The Allens succeeded in having their nascent city designated the seat of government, but they held this prize for only three years. Nevertheless, despite the difficulties of water transportation up the narrow, shallow, and winding Buffalo Bayou, the town prospered with the development of cotton farming in the vicinity.[26]

Galveston, Houston's rival for the cotton trade, enjoyed a more accessible location as a port, for its promoters had selected an island just off the coast. Here they surveyed a huge gridiron street system stretching nearly five miles from one end to the other (Figure 19). The "five or six hundred houses, and about three thousand inhabitants" described in one account of 1840, three years after the city's founding, must have enjoyed ample room. By 1850 Galveston's population had reached five thousand, a figure that doubled in the next decade and continued to increase after the Civil War (Figure 20). Its appearance in 1871 promised that the city would become one of the major urban centers of the South, but Galveston's hopes for a continuation of the rapid rate of development were eventually stifled by hurricane and flood damage from which the town never fully recovered, although it remains a city of substantial size.[27]

These and other future metropolitan centers such as Dallas, surveyed in 1855 (Figure 21), and Fort Worth, laid out about the same time on the site of an abandoned military post (Figure 22), were ventures in private land speculation. Their founders promoted the townsites with methods that had been previously tested in other parts of the United States. Likewise, their original designs possessed no special merit. Some variation of the grid system, with an

26. Adele B. Looscan, "Harris County, 1822–1845, IV: The Beginnings of Houston," *Southwestern Historical Quarterly* 19 (July 1915): 37–64. See also Kenneth W. Wheeler, *To Wear a City's Crown: The Beginnings of Urban Growth in Texas, 1836–1865* (Cambridge, Mass., 1968), for a comparative study of Houston, Galveston, San Antonio, and other Texas cities in the years of independence and early statehood.

27. Perhaps the most interesting document in Galveston's early history is the promotional statement issued in 1837 by the Galveston City Company, led by Michael B. Menard: *City of Galveston, on Galveston Island, in Texas . . . Accompanied with a Plan of the City and Harbor* (New Orleans, 1837). The only copy I have found is in the collection of the Historical Society of Pennsylvania, Philadelphia. The eight-page prospectus concluded with this bit of typical frontier enthusiasm: "No new city or town of the present day, offers anything like the inducements for profitable investment to this. It is like commencing to build another New York, or another New Orleans; and all who embark in it are as certain of realizing great profits, as though they had early engaged in the projection of either of the other places. Now is the time to buy stock in this splendid city. Either stock or lots bought in it, must soon advance one hundred percent."

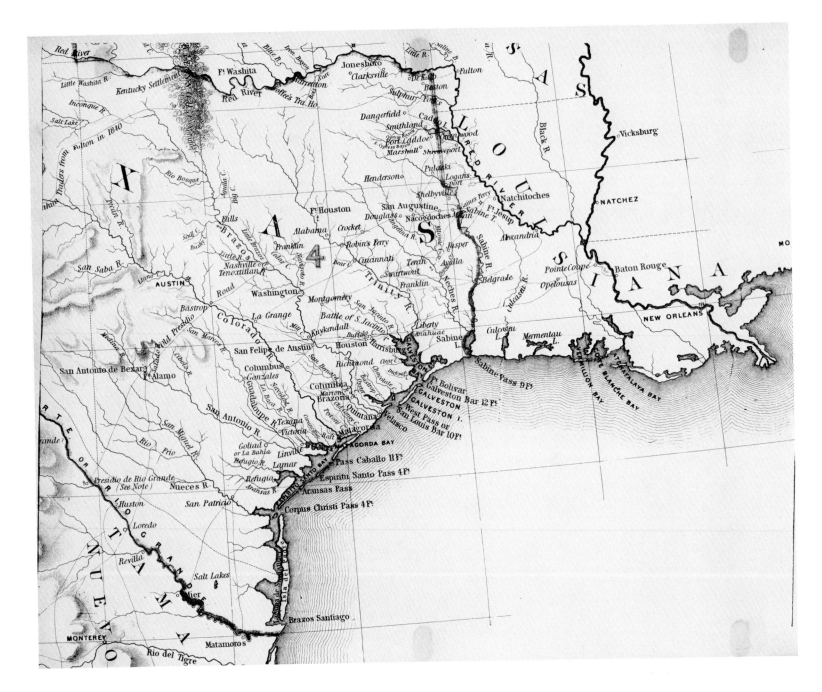

Figure 17. The urban pattern of Texas in 1844

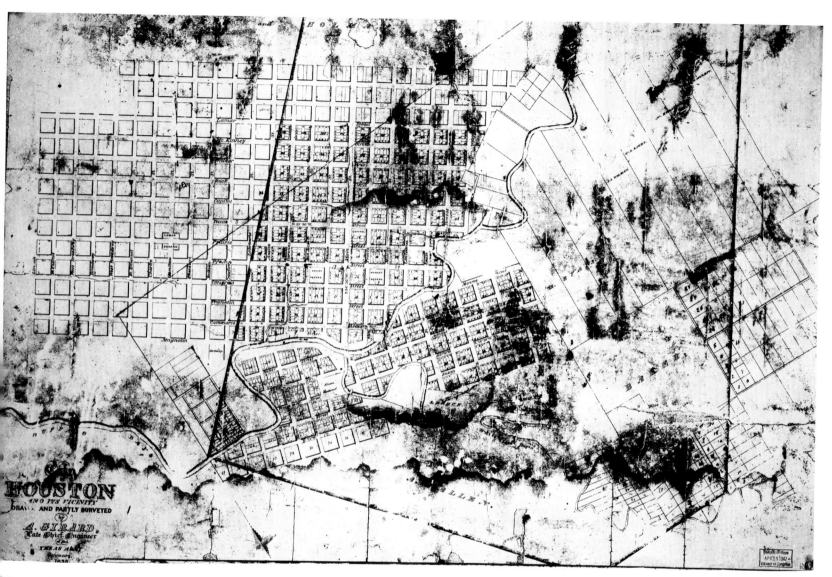

Figure 18. Houston, Texas, in 1839

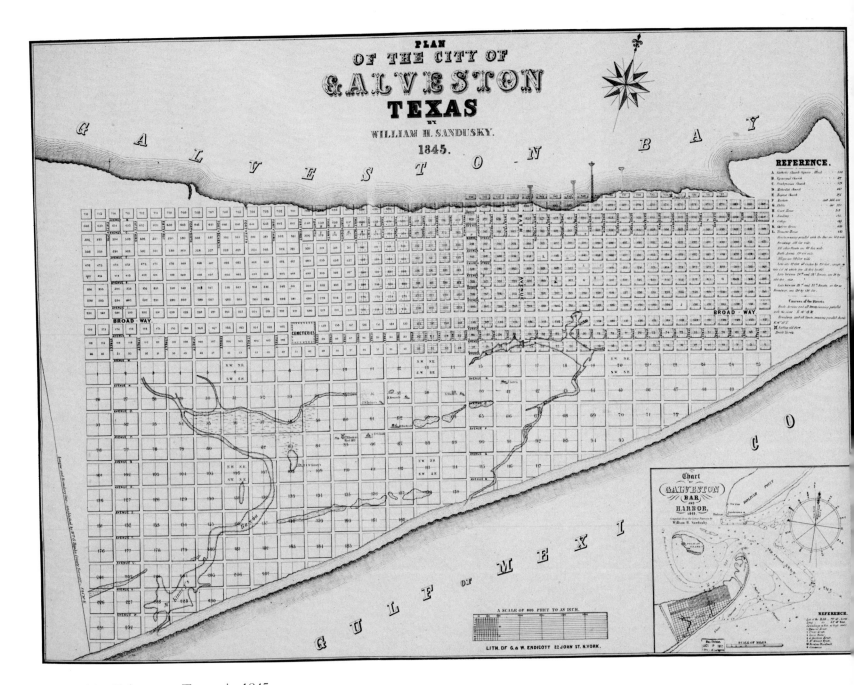

Figure 19. Galveston, Texas, in 1845

ure 20. Galveston, Texas, in 1871

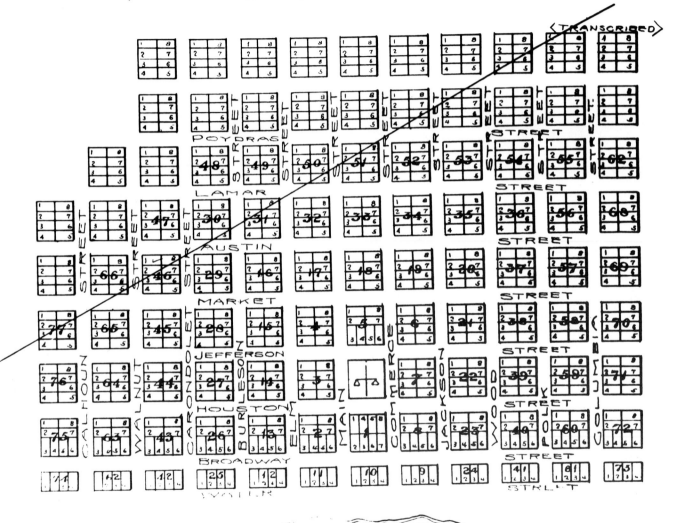

Figure 21. Dallas, Texas, in 1855

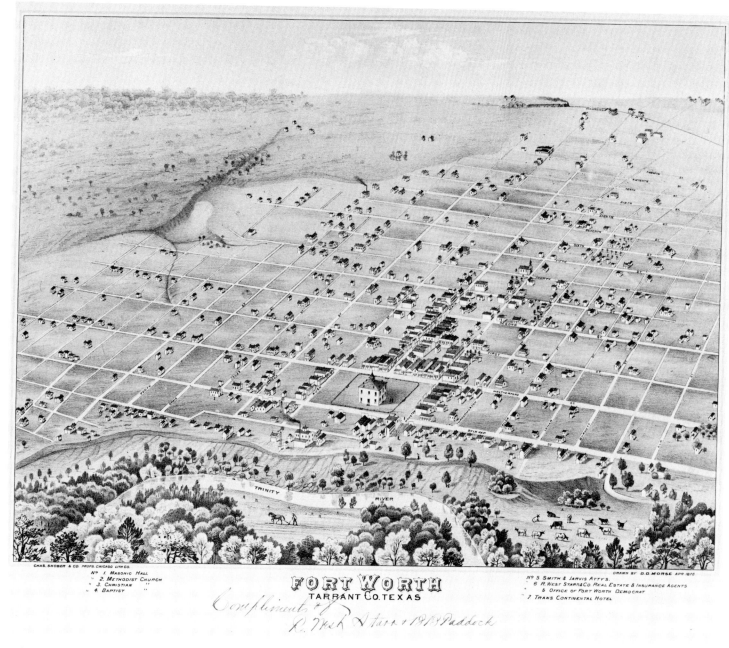

Nº 1. MASONIC HALL
" 2. METHODIST CHURCH
" 3. CHRISTIAN "
" 4. BAPTIST "

FORT WORTH
TARRANT CO. TEXAS

DRAWN BY D.D. MORSE APR. 1876

Nº 5 SMITH & JARVIS ATTY'S.
" 6 R. WEST STARR & CO. REAL ESTATE & INSURANCE AGENTS
& OFFICE OF FORT WORTH DEMOCRAT
" 7 TRANS CONTINENTAL HOTEL

Compliments of
R. West Starr & B.B. Paddock

Figure 22. Fort Worth, Texas, in 1876

occasional block set aside for a courthouse or market or public square, satisfied their proprietors.[28]

The plan of the new national capital of Austin received more care and attention. Officials of the republic of Texas located this city well beyond the closely settled frontier to encourage expansion in an undeveloped region in much the same manner that the site for Brasilia was selected in our own era. Private townsite speculators could scarcely be expected to begin such a project, nor would the usual, unimaginative grid pattern be sufficiently impressive for the seat of government. The government of Texas decided to follow precedents established by the states of North and South Carolina, Georgia, Florida, Ohio, Mississippi, Indiana, and Missouri by undertaking to build the new community as a public enterprise.[29]

Under the direction of President Mirabeau Buonoparte Lamar, Edwin Waller in 1839 acquired the site for Austin and planned the town with a 120-foot-wide central avenue leading up the slope from the Colorado River to a commanding elevation (Figure 23). There Waller located Capitol Square in a frame of sites reserved for future governmental buildings. A street of similar width provided the cross-axis, the western end of which terminated at locations designated for the university and academy. Other public squares, a market, sites for churches, courthouse, jail, penitentiary, armory, and hospital completed the generous allocation of space for civic purposes.[30]

Several other Texas towns resulted from the planning activities in the 1840s of the Adelsverein, a well-organized German colonization society. This group recruited settlers in Europe and sent Prince Carl of Solms-Braunfels to purchase large tracts of land, supervise the surveying of the land, and then distribute it to the settlers. Indianola was planned on Matagorda Bay as the port of entry, and New Braunfels and Fredericksburg were laid out as trading and supply centers to serve the colony's farmlands some thirty miles northeast of San Antonio (Figure 24). The three communities differed in design, with Indianola of least interest. Fredericksburg, planned by John Meusebach, was laid out in a neat linear grid with a rectangular central square. Nicolaus Zink was responsible for the plan of New Braunfels, which has two main streets leading to the midpoints of the sides of an elongated central open space; nearby are sites for marketplace, school, town hall, mill, and church.[31]

In the period following the Civil War the planning of new towns and the

28. A departure from this approach to urban planning in early Texas was for a settlement in what is now Dallas. A group of French utopian followers of Charles Fourier planned La Réunion in 1855 in an intricate pattern of radial avenues and civic spaces. See Reps, *Cities of the American West*, fig. 5.27, p. 149; and George H. Santerre, *White Cliffs of Dallas: The Story of La Réunion, the Old French Colony* (Dallas, 1955). For Dallas, consult Santerre, *Dallas' First Hundred Years, 1856–1956* (Dallas, 1956). For Fort Worth, see Oliver Knight, *Fort Worth: Outpost on the Trinity* (Norman, Okla., 1953).

29. For references to studies on planned capitals in the United States, see John W. Reps, *Monumental Washington: The Planning and Development of the Capital Center* (Princeton, 1967); and works cited in fns. 23 and 24, pp. 24–25, of Reps, "Public Land, Urban Development Policy, and the American Planning Tradition," in Marion Clawson, ed., *Modernizing Urban Land Policy* (Baltimore, 1973).

30. Ernest Winkler, "The Seat of Government of Texas: The Permanent Location of the Seat of Government," *Quarterly of the Texas State Historical Association* 10 (January 1907): 185–245; Ralph Wooster, "Texans Choose a Capital Site," *Texana* 4 (Winter 1966): 351–57; and Alex W. Terrell, "The City of Austin from 1839 to 1865," *Quarterly of the Texas State Historical Association* 14 (October 1910): 113–28.

31. Oscar Haas, *History of New Braunfels and Comal County, Texas, 1844–1946* (Austin, 1968); Rudolph L. Biesele, *History of the German Settlements in Texas, 1831–1861* (Austin, 1930); and Gilbert Giddings Benjamin, *The Germans in Texas: A Study in Immigration* (New York, 1910). There were at least three smaller villages in which members of this group also settled: Sisterdale, Boerne, and Comfort. T. R. Fehrenback, *Lone Star: A History of Texas and the Texans* (New York, 1968), p. 294.

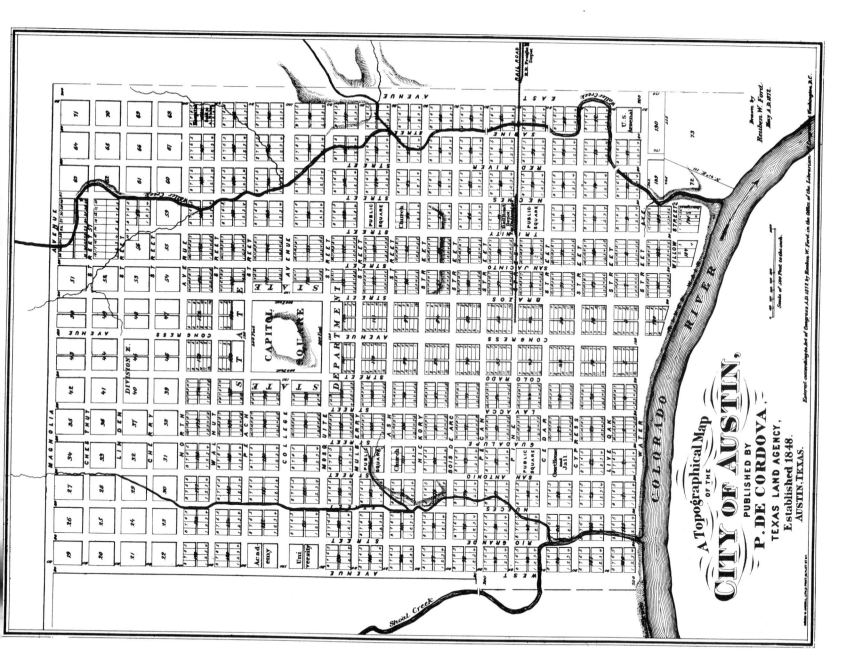

Figure 23. Austin, Texas, as planned in 1839, with additions to 1872

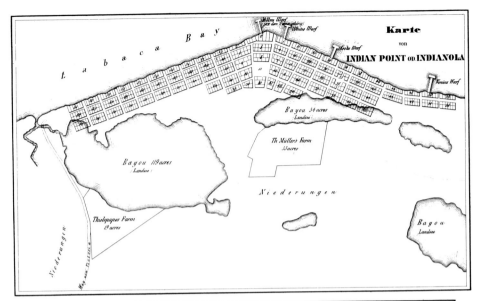

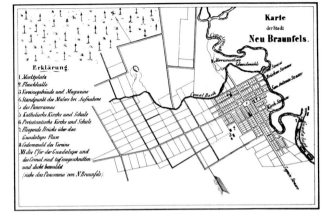

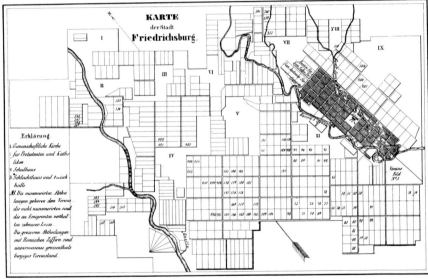

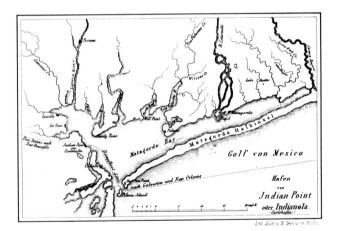

Figure 24. Plans of Indianola, New Braunfels, and Fredericksburg, Texas, and a map of Matagorda Bay, circa 1850

32. N. C. Abbott, *Lincoln: Name and Place, Nebraska State Historical Society Publications* 21 (1930): 1–133; and A. B. Hayes and Samuel D. Cox, *History of the City of Lincoln* (Lincoln, Nebr., 1889).

33. Hallock F. Raup, "Anaheim: A German Community of Frontier California," *American German Review* 12 (December 1945): 7–11; and Mildred Y. MacArthur, *Anaheim "The Mother Colony"* (Los Angeles, 1959). See also Oscar O. Winther, "The Colony System of Southern California," *Agricultural History* 27 (July 1953): 94–103.

34. Lyman Wight led a group of Mormons to Austin in 1845 and then moved on to found the town of Zodiac in 1847 a few miles from Fredericksburg. Davis Bitton, "Mormons in Texas: The Ill-Fated Lyman Wight Colony, 1844–1858," *Arizona and the West* 11 (Spring 1969): 5–26.

expansion or decline of existing cities in Texas were closely related to the development of railroad transportation, a subject that will be treated here in terms of the ways in which it affected urbanization in other regions of the West. But what occurred in Texas through the decade of the 1850s was a microcosm of similar events elsewhere. The planned development under public sponsorship of the Texas capital was an achievement duplicated with equally impressive results in the founding of Lincoln, Nebraska, in 1867.[32] Colonization societies were responsible for a number of planned towns in other states, including Greeley, Colorado, and Anaheim, California.[33] Small utopian groups with plans far greater than their resources or organizational abilities created short-lived communities throughout the West. Even the enormous achievement of the Mormons in Utah was preceded by a short, abortive effort by a few members of that church to establish themselves in Texas.[34]

Most characteristic, however, was urban planning as a tool of the land speculator. In this context, it was Texas that provided the earliest Western proving ground for the techniques in town promotion that had been used by earlier real estate entrepreneurs in the East and Midwest. It was not long before other parts of the West would be occupied by additional settlers, and, as in Texas, town founders and land speculators led the way.

FRONTIER SETTLEMENTS OF THE PACIFIC NORTHWEST

While many of the Americans flocking to Texas came from nearby states, settlers traveling to Oregon in the 1840s were faced with a long and arduous trip. Most of them came by land, following a trail that led westward from the Missouri River along the Platte River through the Nebraska plains, up the valley of the North Platte to South Pass in Wyoming, and down the Snake River to the Columbia. At The Dalles, these pioneers put their wagons on rafts and floated down the Columbia to the mouth of the Willamette River, settling in the fertile Willamette River valley, which extended 150 miles or so to the south.

Information about this attractive region had trickled back to the East from early explorers and fur traders. A few dedicated missionaries had established their posts in the Willamette valley as early as 1834, and nearby they planted some of the land to wheat. At Champoeg, some twenty miles above the falls of the river, the earliest nucleated settlement gradually took form. It consisted of a trading post, several warehouses, stores, and a number of houses. Here the few Yankee settlers marketed their grain and hides, most of which passed through the hands of the English Hudson's Bay Company, whose chief factor, John McLoughlin, controlled most of the trade in a region where England and the United States contended for political dominance.[35]

In an effort to confine American settlement to the area south of the Columbia, McLoughlin in the winter of 1842–1843 surveyed a townsite at the falls of the Willamette, a few miles above its mouth, and offered free lots to all settlers. His town of Oregon City consisted of a single street. Slightly angled at its midpoint to follow the curving riverbank, this street provided access to the nine rectangular blocks on each side. Four years later McLoughlin enlarged the town by adding a much larger and more regular grid with a broad avenue dividing the two parts at one end and with a public square at the center of the expanded community (Figure 25).

At the end of its first year, a visitor described Oregon City as consisting of "fifty-three buildings . . . among which were four stores, four mills . . . , one public-house, one black-smith's shop and various other mechanics' shops; a church was also . . . commenced." Growth continued, and by 1847 another observer referred to Oregon City as a "bustling little village . . . with its neatly-painted white houses, and its six or seven hundred inhabitants."[36] A year later, after the settlement of the boundary issue with England in 1846, Oregon City became the capital of the territory, serving in this capacity until 1851.

However, even an expanded Oregon City could not accommodate the increasing number of settlers arriving via the Oregon Trail. In a short time a dozen or more new towns were surveyed by other townsite developers. Linn City in 1843, Linnton and Multnomah City the following year, Falls City in 1845, Milwaukie in 1847, and several others, including Green Point and Clackamas City, soon lined the banks of the Willamette near or below its falls.

35. For the development of Champoeg, see Barth, *Instant Cities*, pp. 80–91; and John A. Hussey, *Champoeg: Place of Transition* (Portland, 1967). A helpful biography of McLoughlin is Richard Montgomery, *The White-Headed Eagle: John McLoughlin, Builder of an Empire* (New York, 1935)

36. Lansford W. Hastings, *The Emigrant's Guide to Oregon and California* (Cincinnati, 1845), p. 56; and J. Quinn Thornton, *Oregon and California in 1848* (New York, 1849), 2: 287. Thornton visited Oregon City in 1847.

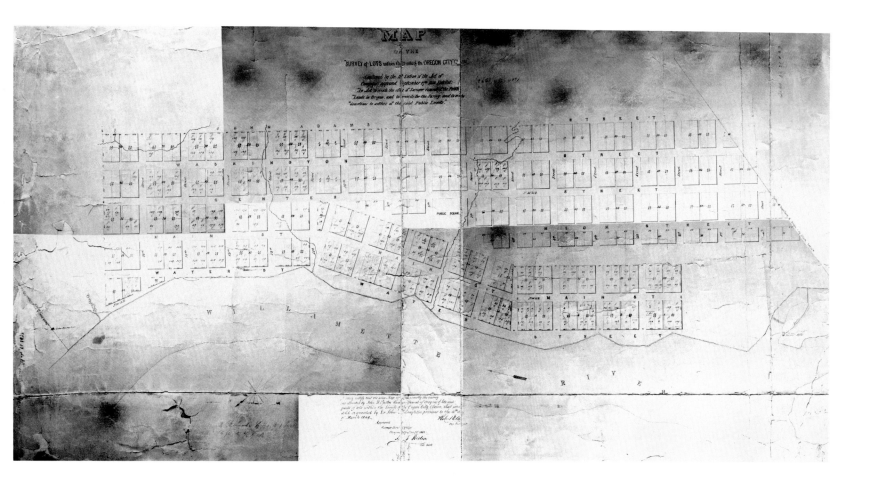

Figure 25. Oregon City, Oregon, in 1849

Farther up the river, Salem (Figure 26) and Eugene in 1846 and Albany and Corvallis in 1848 joined the growing list of communities dotting the map of Oregon before midcentury.

What was to become the most important city in Oregon and one of the great cities of the American West also began its existence at this time. Asa Lovejoy and Francis Pettygrove selected its site in 1845 and engaged Thomas Brown to lay it out in a linear grid on the left bank of the Willamette about halfway between Oregon City and the Columbia River. Pettygrove, a native of Maine, won the toss of a coin to determine which of the partners could name the new town, and Portland it became. Their plan could not have been simpler: a single sixty-foot street, crossed at right angles by seven others, which divided the site into sixteen blocks of identical size, each having eight lots.

As additional settlers arrived, the proprietors subdivided adjacent land. Their first extension added a group of six blocks to the north and a third tier of blocks inland extending the full length of the expanded town (Figure 27). Between the north and south sections they reserved two large tracts, each equal in size to two blocks. Although in the fall of 1846 Portland could be described as having only "twelve or 15 new homes . . . already occupied, and others building," it was not long before a much more rapid period of growth began.[37]

A new arrival in November 1850 observed "under way not less than 150 new houses." Earlier that fall and the preceding summer "there . . . [were] . . . built over 100 dwellings . . . eighteen stores, six public boarding houses . . . [and] . . . two large churches."[38] Two years before that time, Portland's new proprietor, Daniel Lownsdale, had enlarged the town by platting additional blocks along the waterfront, extending its grid along the river to the north, and subdividing a large area inland (Figure 28).

Lownsdale provided two blocks near the center of Portland as public squares and at its western edge laid out a tier of eleven narrow blocks as a park. In later years, as Portland continued to grow, this park strip was extended north and south (Figure 29). Although some of these blocks were eventually disposed of for building purposes, a ribbon of them remains as a kind of inner greenbelt within the central city. It was a generous and unusual

37. From a description by Lt. Neil Howison, as quoted in Eugene E. Snyder, *Early Portland, Stump-Town Triumphant: Rival Towns on the Willamette, 1831–1854* (Portland, Ore., 1970), p. 37. Snyder's book is an excellent study of frontier town promotion and the urban rivalry that characterized much of the early West.

38. Quoted from an unidentified source in Charles H. Carey, *A General History of Oregon Prior to 1861* (Portland, Ore., 1935), 2: 655.

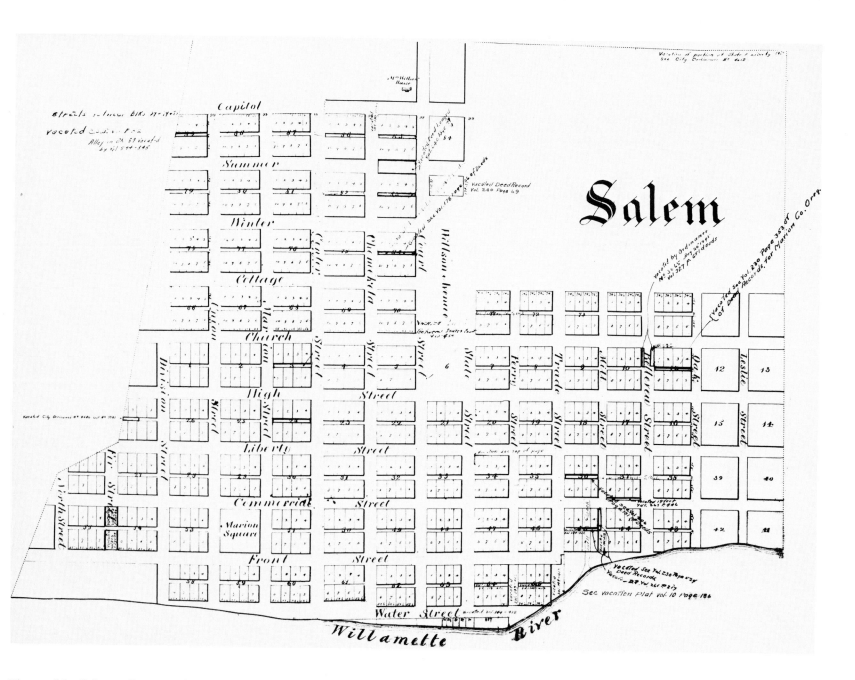

Figure 26. Salem, Oregon, in 1850

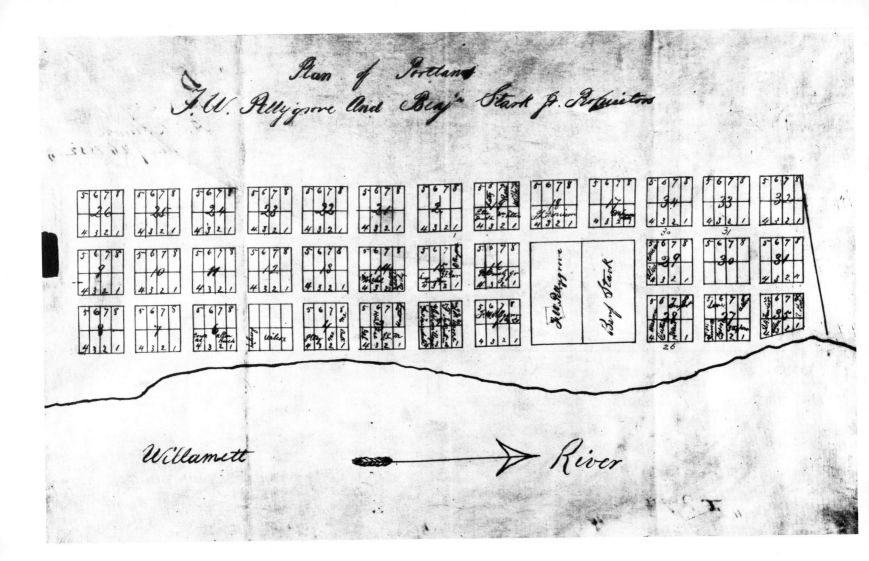

Figure 27. Portland, Oregon, in 1845

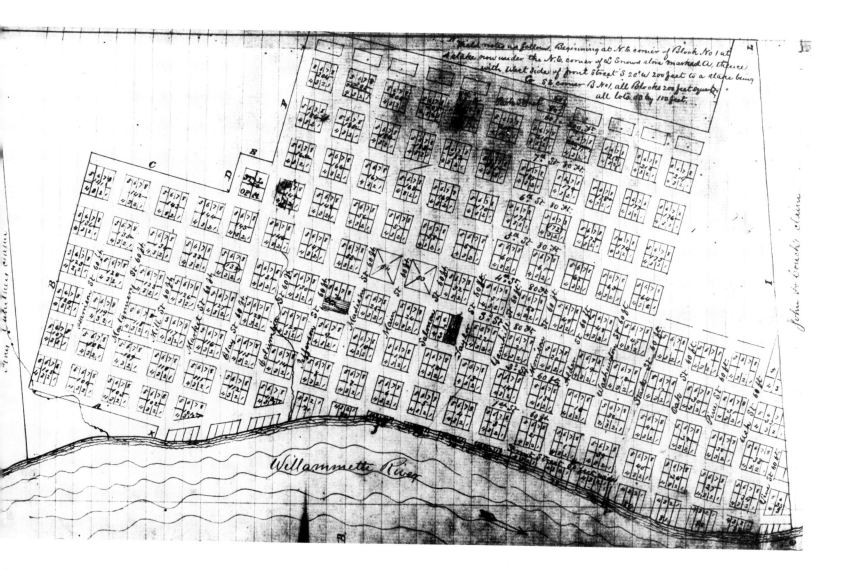

Figure 28. Portland, Oregon, in 1848

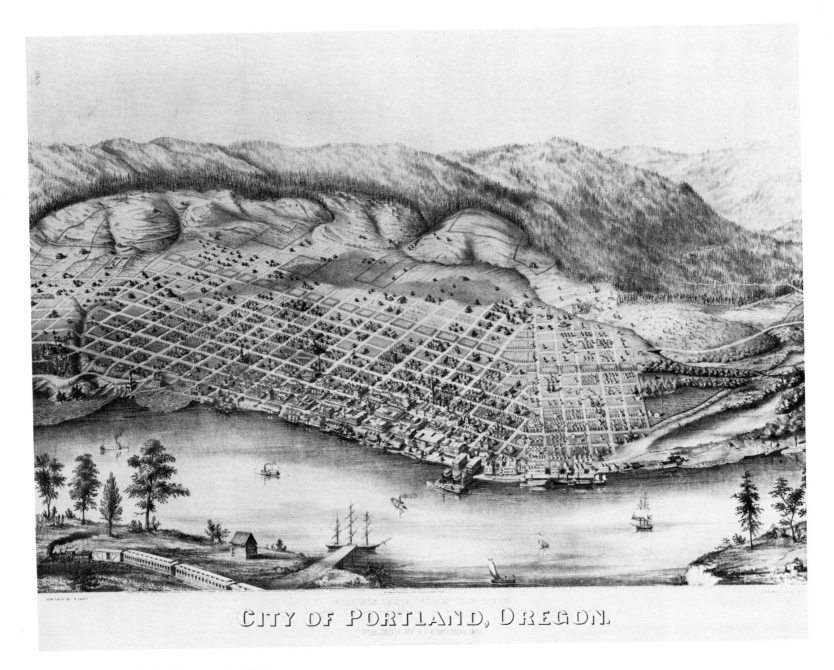

CITY OF PORTLAND, OREGON.

Figure 29. Portland, Oregon, in 1870

39. For plans of Louisville showing tiers of open blocks not unlike those of Portland, see John W. Reps, *The Making of Urban America: A History of City Planning in the United States* (Princeton, 1965), figs. 125 and 126, pp. 213 and 215. In addition to the early Oregon towns mentioned in the text, there were many others—not all of them successful. Brief accounts of them can be found in Howard Corning, "Ghost Towns on the Willamette of the Riverboat Period," *Oregon Historical Quarterly* 48 (June 1947): 55–67.

40. Carey, *Oregon*, 2: 734–35.

41. Address by Judge William Strong, as quoted in ibid., 2: 659. Astoria's early history is traced in Grace P. Morris, "Development of Astoria, 1811–1850," *Oregon Historical Quarterly* 38 (December 1937): 413–24.

42. Edmund S. Meany, "First American Settlement on the Puget Sound," *Washington Historical Quarterly* 7 (April 1916): 135–43; and "Edmund Sylvester's Narrative of the Founding of Olympia," *Pacific Northwest Quarterly* 36 (October 1945): 331–99.

43. "Henry Yesler and the Founding of Seattle," *Pacific Northwest Quarterly* 42 (October 1951): 271–76.

legacy, but Lownsdale's motives remain unclear. He may have borrowed the idea from his native Kentucky, where Louisville once had a similar arrangement of public parks. Or he may have intended these open blocks to serve as a firebreak for a town on a heavily wooded location and with only the most primitive fire-fighting equipment.[39]

Elsewhere in Oregon town promoters platted new towns to rival those of the Willamette valley. On the south bank of the Columbia, Henry Knighton in 1850 laid out St. Helens, named for his native town in Lancashire (Figure 30). Although its plan followed the usual grid pattern, four large public squares and a two-block-long open space on the waterfront provided potential civic focal points and suggested that the proprietor of St. Helens had some knowledge of town-planning principles.[40]

Knighton expected St. Helens to flourish as a major port, but navigation of the Columbia by sailing vessels proved difficult, and although the town survived, it failed to live up to the hopes of its founder. A somewhat older town, Astoria, had a similar experience. Planned in 1844 near the mouth of the Columbia by John Shively, it, too, had a grid plan that featured a number of square and circular open spaces (Figure 31). An early arrival noted in 1850, however, that only "upon the map" could one find the "avenues and streets, squares and public parks, wharves and warehouses, churches, schools and theaters" promised by its promoter. Astoria then, he said, was a mere "straggling hamlet consisting of a dozen or so small houses, irregularly planted along the river bank, shut in by the dense forest."[41]

After the right to settle north of the Columbia River had been established, American town developers ventured into this area to plan new communities. Olympia, which later became the capital, dates from 1850, and the following year Steilacoom and Fort Townsend were planned in little grid patterns, the latter under the direction of Francis Pettygrove, who had unwisely sold out his interest in Portland.[42]

Seattle had equally humble origins. Located on the shore of Elliott Bay on the east side of Puget Sound, the town began in 1852 with a single street crossed by five others. The townsite company had greater ambitions, however, and by the end of 1853 it had extended the original streets and added many others (Figure 32). A public square faced a triangular open space into which the two main streets led.[43]

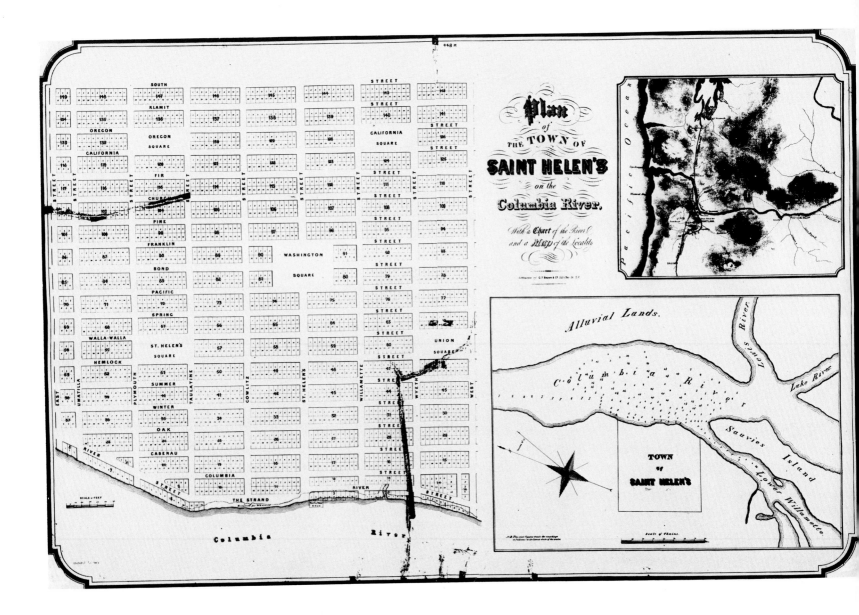

Figure 30. St. Helens, Oregon, circa 1875

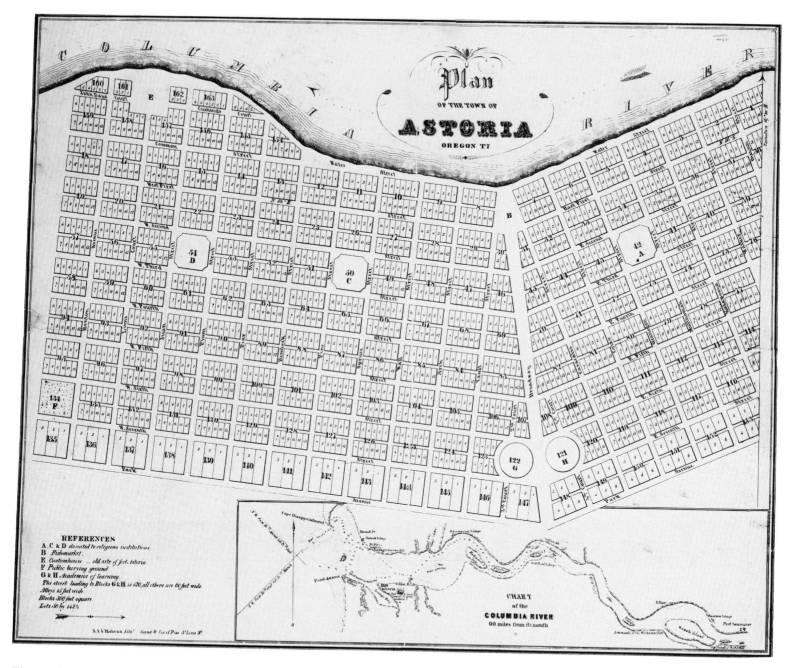

Figure 31. Astoria, Oregon, circa 1850

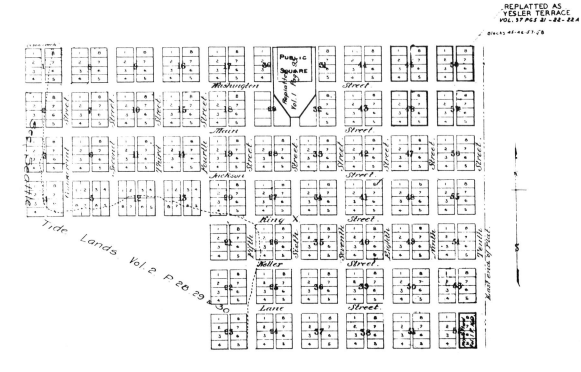

Plat of the
Town of Seattle
King County, Washington Territory.

Figure 32. Seattle, Washington, in 1853

44. For the development of Seattle, see Clarence B. Bagley, *History of Seattle from the Earliest Settlement to the Present Time*, 3 vols. (Chicago, 1916).

45. Priscilla Knuth, "'Picturesque' Frontier: The Army's Fort Dalles," *Oregon Historical Quarterly* 68 (December 1966): 293–333, and (March 1967): 5–52; Howard McKinley Corning, ed., *Dictionary of Oregon History . . .* (Portland, Ore., 1956), p. 241; and Carey, *Oregon*, 2: 670.

46. D. W. Meinig, *The Great Columbia Plain: A Historical Geography, 1805–1910* (Seattle, 1968), pp. 201–4; Martha J. Lamb, "A Glimpse of the Valley of Many Waters," *Magazine of American History* 12 (September 1884): 193–210. An earlier community also began its existence adjacent to a fortlike compound. This was Vancouver, Washington, where in 1850 Amos Short surveyed land previously claimed by Henry Williamson into a clumsy grid of streets striking the bank of the Columbia River at sharp angles. Its only graceful feature was the long strip reserved as a boat landing. This has survived in the modern city as a handsome park at the edge of the business district. For plans of early Vancouver and the Hudson's Bay trading post and fort, see John A. Hussey, *The History of Fort Vancouver and Its Physical Structure* (Tacoma, Wash., 1957).

When gold was discovered on the Fraser River in Canada in 1858, Seattle prospered as a supply and outfitting center for many persons bound for the mines. Although this did not provide a lasting reason for economic or population growth, the facilities of Seattle's harbor soon had to be expanded to accommodate increased shipments of lumber from the nearby forests (Figure 33). The decision in 1861 to locate in Seattle what became the University of Washington helped to stimulate further expansion, and by the end of the 1870s Seattle had cast its network of streets well beyond the original nucleus of the early town.[44]

While the earliest communities in the Pacific Northwest were concentrated on the Willamette and lower Columbia rivers and along the shores of Puget Sound, it was not long before they were joined by other towns to the east. At The Dalles, where Oregon settlers left the dusty trail to transfer their belongings to rafts, a nucleated settlement developed in the vicinity of Fort Lee. In 1855 officials of Wasco County ordered the place formally surveyed into a grid of twenty-four blocks and straight streets.[45]

Many miles east of The Dalles the U.S. army had located a post in the valley of the Walla Walla River at the time of the Indian Wars of 1855–1858. Near the military tract settlers began to erect houses when the conflict ceased. After the mining boom began at nearby Orofino in Idaho, the town was incorporated as Walla Walla and laid out in the usual frontier grid (Figure 34). The street plan fitted uncomfortably into the government survey system, but this did not prevent the early prosperity of the new town, whose merchants were kept busy supplying miners in the northern Idaho gold district.[46]

BONANZA TOWNS OF THE MINING FRONTIER

As the first towns of Oregon were passing through their pioneer period, a new and much larger frontier of urbanization opened to the south when gold was discovered in California. Beginning with the influx of tens of thousands of adventurers and prospectors in 1849, dozens of mining camps, several major supply centers, and one great economic and social capital sprang into exis-

Figure 33. Seattle, Washington, in 1878

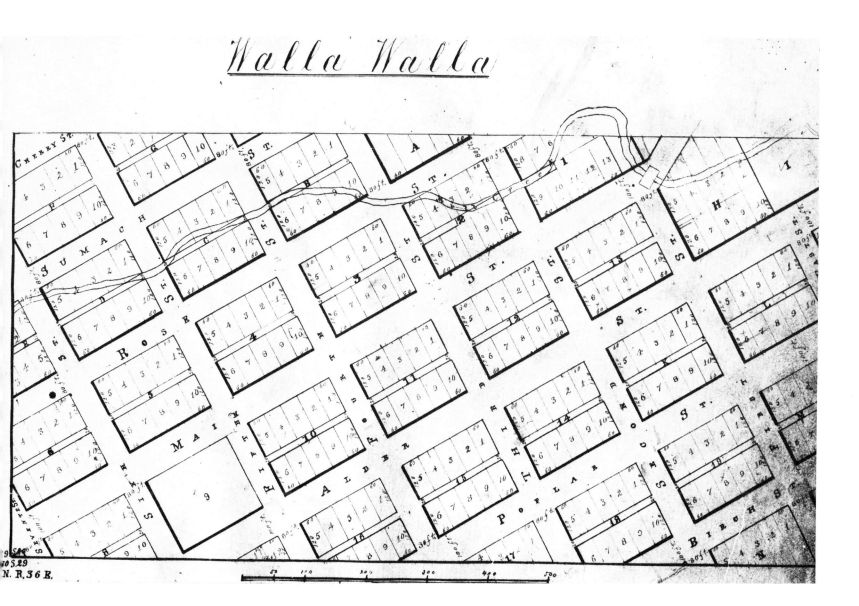

Figure 34. Walla Walla, Washington, in 1865

tence almost overnight. Many of the camps did not survive long, and few of those in California had any features that might be dignified under the title of a plan. However, in such places as Coloma, Sonora, and Grass Valley, hastily created provisional town governments made some efforts—not always entirely successful—to survey streets, remove encroaching structures, and establish regulations governing land titles and conflicting claims.[47]

A view of Grass Valley in 1852, for example, presents a picture quite at variance with the generally held image of California mining camps as scenes of total disorder (Figure 35). Three years after the first gold strike, when mining operations still continued unabated, the buildings in Grass Valley's business district had uniform street frontages, and in the adjoining residential quarter one can see tidy, fenced yards and adequately spaced houses.[48]

In the most important mining town in Nevada—the great silver center of Virginia City—the first street was surveyed shortly after miners began arriving on the scene in 1859. New streets were soon laid out in closely spaced parallel ranks extending down the steep slopes of Mount Davidson. In 1865 the town government proudly adopted an official map for what was by that time a large and prosperous community (Figure 36).[49]

Additional examples of planning in the mining towns can be found in other parts of the bonanza frontier. Some kind of survey was made of Central City, Colorado, shortly after John Gregory discovered gold at the site in 1859, although the oldest surviving drawing dates from 1863. Hal Sayre laid out the streets following the winding valley floors of Gregory, Nevada, and Eureka gulches, making others at higher elevations roughly parallel to those below (Figure 37). It was no triumph of planning, but it provided the basic structure for this community at an early date.[50]

At Helena, Montana, thousands of miners crowded the narrow valley of Last Chance Gulch when gold was discovered in July 1864. That fall the town's new citizens met to organize a town government and delegated authority to three commissioners to survey the townsite and to "make such laws and regulations as may be deemed necessary, to regulate the location and size of lots, streets, alleys, etc."[51]

The official plat of Helena drawn in 1868 doubtless reflects the decisions of the commissioners (Figure 38). Some of the irregularities of the plan may be

47. For such activities in Sonora, see Thomas R. Stoddart, *Annals of Tuolumne County* (Sonora, Calif., 1963), p. 104, and Edna B. Buckbee, *The Saga of Old Tuolumne* (New York, 1935), p. 30.

48. A street plan of Grass Valley of about 1852 is reproduced in Reps, *Cities of the American West*, fig. 7.8, p. 205. See also fig. 7.4, p. 200, for a map of Coloma in 1857 showing two straight, parallel streets intersected by several others at right angles.

49. The best contemporary description of Virginia City, not always flattering, can be found in J. Ross Browne, *A Peep at Washoe and Washoe Revisited* (Balboa Island, Calif., 1959), a reprint of some of his journalistic accounts of the time.

50. Several later Colorado mining towns were planned at or soon after the beginning of settlement, including Idaho Springs, Georgetown, Leadville, and Cripple Creek. All of these are discussed at length, with maps and views, in Reps, *Cities of the American West*, pp. 457–89.

51. For the complete text of the resolutions adopted at that time, see Joaquin Miller, *An Illustrated History of the State of Montana* (Chicago, 1894), pp. 272–74.

GRASS VALLEY, NEVADA COUNTY.
CALIFORNIA.

Figure 35. Grass Valley, California, in 1852

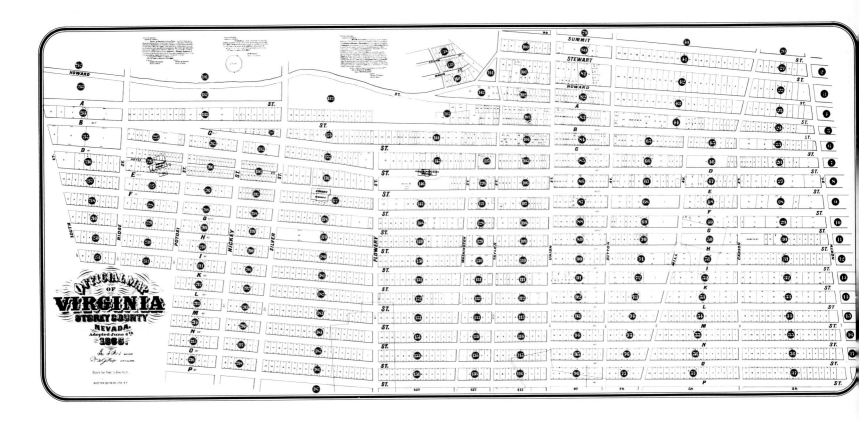

Figure 36. Official map of Virginia City, Nevada, in 1865

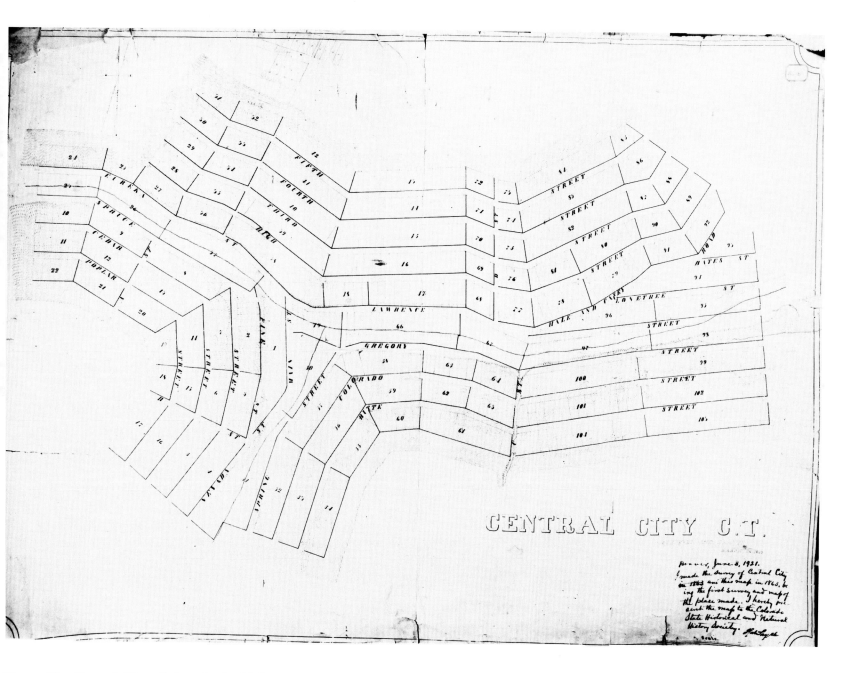

Figure 37. Central City, Colorado, in 1863

Figure 38. Helena, Montana, in 1868

52. For additional details concerning Helena, Virginia City, and several other examples of planned mining towns in Idaho, Montana, and South Dakota, see Reps, *Cities of the American West*, pp. 491–522.

53. I have summarized this rather surprising aspect of American planning with additional examples in John W. Reps, "Bonanza Towns: Urban Planning on the Western Mining Frontier," in Ralph Ehrenberg, ed., *Pattern and Process: Research in Historical Geography* (Washington, D.C., 1975), pp. 271–89. Several reproductions of early plans and views of planned mining communities are included. My conclusions at least partially refute the popular notion that all of the mining towns somehow took form spontaneously in an atmosphere of unfettered private decisionmaking over such urban elements as streets, public sites, lot sizes, and so forth. This is another example of the transplanting of "Eastern" values to the American West, and it challenges at still another point the Turner thesis of the frontier as a place where new and distinctive patterns of social and political behavior were developed.

54. For a thorough, informative, and well-documented study of the Western mining frontier, see William S. Greever, *The Bonanza West: The Story of the Western Mining Rushes, 1848–1900* (Norman, Okla., 1963). A much earlier analysis of the development of governmental institutions in the mining towns first appeared in 1885 but has been republished with editorial notes by Joseph Henry Jackson. See Charles H. Shinn, *Mining Camps: A Study in American Frontier Government* (New York, 1948). For the literature of the California mining era, consult Carl I. Wheat, *Books of the California Gold Rush* (San Francisco, 1949).

the result of topography, although most of them probably represent accommodations by the planners to sites already occupied and so substantially built up that the buildings could not be removed.

Far more regular was the design surveyed in 1868 for Virginia City, Montana, five years after a rich lode of gold brought thousands of miners to the site at Alder Gulch (Figure 39). J. L. Corbett's plan included a location for the territorial capitol, in addition to three parks and three cemeteries—all set in a huge street grid covering almost a square mile.[52]

This sequence of a town plan following soon after the discovery of mineral wealth and the influx of miners was repeated in many other mining centers of the West, indicating that the desire for some kind of urban order, however primitive, was deeply instilled in the minds of those who flocked to the sites of new discoveries. At Austin and American City, Nevada; Idaho Springs, Georgetown, Leadville, and Cripple Creek, Colorado; and Custer City and Deadwood, South Dakota, among many other places, streets, blocks, and lots were planned by committees of miners or by surveyors employed by the first town governments at the earliest stages of community formation.[53]

In the mining camps urban land was far less important as a source of profit than gold and silver, but in such supply and outfitting centers as Sacramento, Stockton, and Marysville, California; Denver, Colorado; Boise, Idaho; and Benton, Bozeman, and Missoula, Montana, real estate development and speculation proved popular and profitable. These and other towns were planned by entrepreneurs who recognized opportunities that were far less risky, with greater potential for long-term profit, and involving fewer hardships than scrambling through the Sierra or Rocky mountains with a prospector's pick and pan.[54]

The two most important of these supply centers today are Sacramento and Denver. Both were provided with extensive gridiron street plans that permitted substantial population growth before additions were required. They, like the mining camps and other distribution points along the early gold and silver frontiers, existed as established communities well before the agricultural development of their hinterlands.

Sacramento's plan was the work of Capt. William Warner and the son of John Sutter, whose fortlike trading center stood near the mouth of the Ameri-

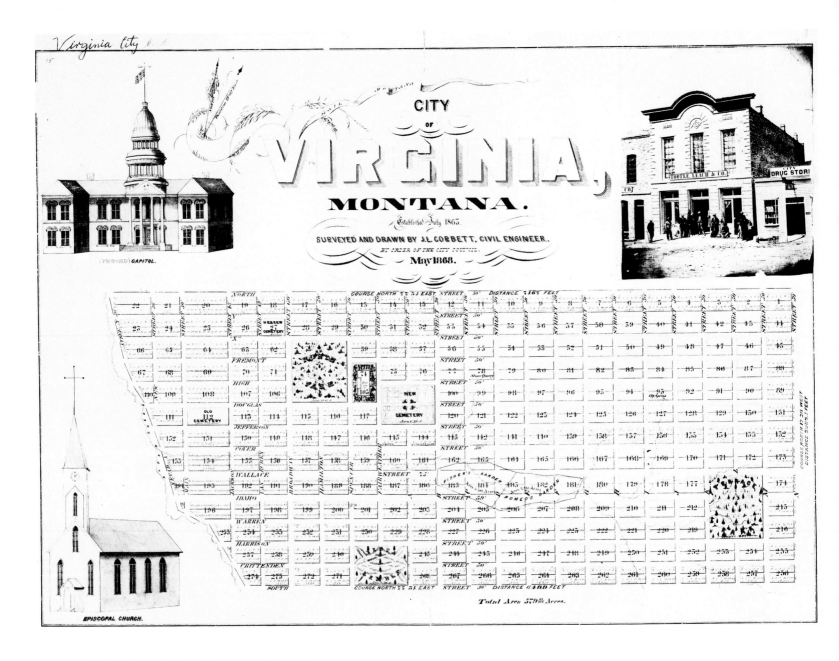

Figure 39. Virginia City, Montana, in 1868

55. McCarver had previously been involved in the planning and development of Burlington and McCarverstown, Iowa, and, in partnership with Burnett, Linnton, Oregon. See Michael B. Husband, "Morton M. McCarver: An Iowa Entrepreneur in the Far West," *Annals of Iowa* 40 (Spring 1970): 241–54. Later he planned Commencement City, Washington, which was eventually embraced by the City of Tacoma.

56. Burnett left an account of the Sacramento real estate promotion. See Peter H. Burnett, *An Old California Pioneer* (Oakland, Calif., 1946), pp. 171–75. A valuable study, well illustrated, of Sacramento's early years is Aubrey V. Neasham and James E. Henley, *The City of the Plain: Sacramento in the Nineteenth Century* (Sacramento, Calif., 1969). For Sacramento's rival as a supply center in the northern mining area of California, see Earl Ramey, "The Beginnings of Marysville," *California Historical Society Quarterly* 14 (September 1935): 194–229, and (December 1935): 375–407. Not all of the California town-promotion schemes were successful. Benicia was one virtual failure, although the town managed to survive. Boston and Toualome City disappeared altogether. The story of another can be found in Ernest A. Wiltsee, "The City of New York of the Pacific," *California Historical Society Quarterly* 12 (March 1933): 24–34.

57. The most recent history of Denver is Lyle Dorset, *The Queen City: A History of Denver* (Boulder, 1977). Barth's *Instant Cities* focuses more sharply on Denver's early years. Older but still valuable is Nolie Mumey, *History of the Early Settlements of Denver (1599–1860)* (Glendale, Calif., 1959). An eyewitness account is Henry Villard, *The Past and Present of the Pike's Peak Gold Regions* (1860; Reprint, Princeton, 1932). The later development of Denver in the railroad era, along with similar treatment of other major Western urban

can River where it entered the Sacramento River. The two were doubtless aided by Sutter's attorney, Peter Burnett, and the latter's friend and onetime town promotion associate in Oregon, Morton McCarver. Many of the ideas for Sacramento may well have come from McCarver, an experienced townsite developer from the Midwest who, like many others, brought to the West all of the techniques of urban land development that had been thoroughly tested on older frontiers of settlement.[55]

The Sacramento grid was constructed of eighty-foot streets, with only M Street, one hundred feet wide, departing from this uniform standard (Figure 40). The planners reserved twelve of the blocks for public squares. Their even distribution and uniform size suggest that the founders had little idea where the center of the enormous city might develop. While most of the early purchasers selected lots near the fort standing some distance from the river, the most intensive growth could be found along the waterfront (Figure 41).

By the summer of 1849 lots that a few months earlier had sold for $250 were bringing $3,000. The younger Sutter adroitly gave away some of the lots to attract merchants needed to assure commercial diversity. This was standard practice in the East, and it proved as successful in Sacramento, promoting the city's speedy growth and enriching Sutter and his associates in the process. A view of Sacramento in 1857 (Figure 42) reveals the remarkably rapid tempo of urban development that transformed General Sutter's pastoral landscape to a large and modern city in less than a decade.[56]

Denver's origins were less orderly. During the summer and fall of 1858, no fewer than five townsite companies staked out conflicting claims to the site where Cherry Creek entered the South Platte River. These eventually dwindled to three: Denver and Auraria, bitter rivals divided by Cherry Creek, and Highland, occupying the opposite bank of the South Platte (Figure 43). Although the failure of Cherry Creek to yield more than traces of gold depressed real estate values for a time, the big strikes in the mountains a year later brought instant prosperity to property owners. Town lots soon were changing hands at more than twenty times their original prices.[57]

Like that of Sacramento, Denver's plan fell far short of being a masterpiece of urban design. It lacked a central focus, there was no provision for parks or civic spaces, and each street on the plat appeared very much like the others.

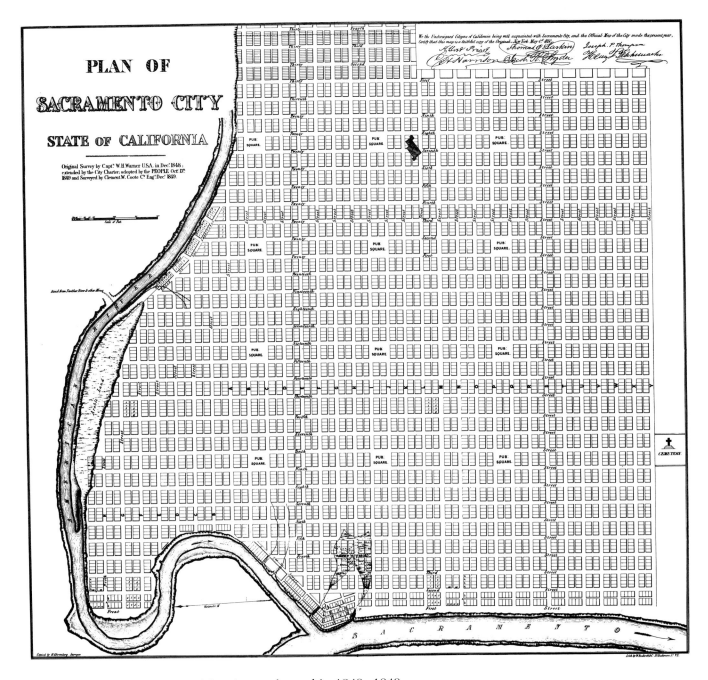

Figure 40. Sacramento, California, as planned in 1848–1849

Figure 41. Sacramento, California, in 1849

Figure 42. Sacramento, California, in 1857

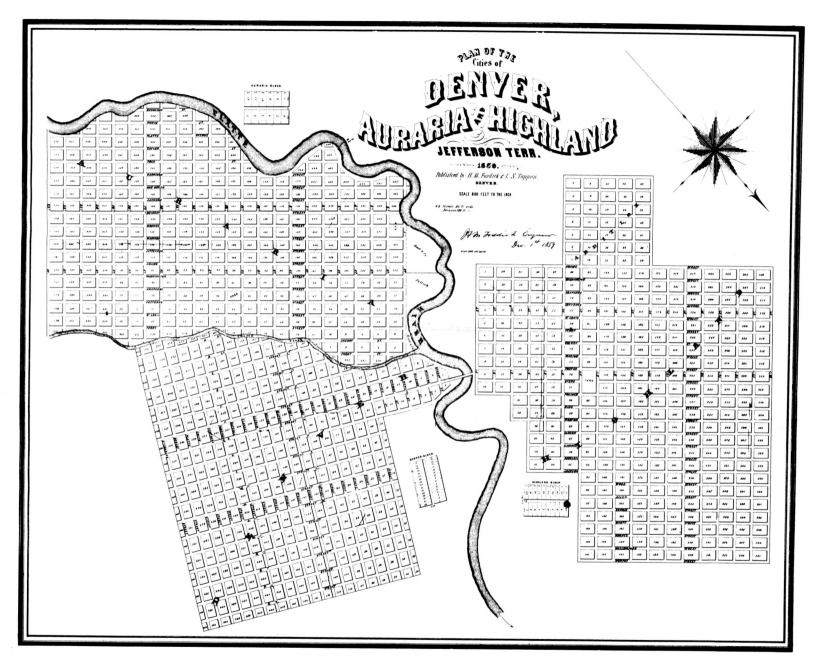

Figure 43. Denver, Colorado, in 1859

Yet like its California counterpart, the city quickly developed an urban character that closely resembled urban areas in the long-settled portions of the country. Less than ten years after the founding of Denver, a French mining engineer was astonished to find many "attractive" houses, "churches, whose number already exceeds the half dozen," and "wide streets, quite open, watered [and] planted with trees" (Figure 44). He noted that "the movement of life is everywhere" and concluded with astonishment that "one would hardly believe himself at the end of the prairies, 2,000 miles from New York."[58]

The planning of Denver, of several other towns along the base of the Rockies, and of the many mining towns in the rugged mountain area created a new urban frontier some 250 miles west of the line of settlement that by the late 1850s ran through the eastern third of Kansas and Nebraska and included a smaller portion of the Dakotas along the borders of Iowa and Minnesota. Here, too, beginning with the opening of Kansas and Nebraska to white occupancy, cities were planned before plows broke the plains.

PLANNING ON THE PLAINS

Even before President Pierce signed the Kansas and Nebraska Act in May 1854, groups of land speculators and townsite developers in neighboring Missouri and Iowa busied themselves scouting out prospective city locations and organizing corporate enterprises. In the summer of 1854 the western bank of the Missouri River swarmed with land surveyors staking out streets for dozens of towns in the three-hundred-mile stretch of river north of Kansas City.

Seemingly, each new town had a newspaper, and their columns were full of such announcements as that appearing in the 15 July issue of the *Nebraska Palladium* trumpeting the achievements and immodest expectations of the Bellevue Town Company: "Within the last month a large city upon a grand scale has been laid out, with a view of the location of the capital of Nebraska, at this point, and with a view to making it the center of commerce, and the half-way house between the Atlantic and Pacific Oceans."[59]

Bellevue occupied a site near a fur-trading post, government Indian Agency headquarters, and missionary establishment (Figure 45). Florence was planned on a location used some years earlier as a way station on the Mormon migration to Utah from Nauvoo, Illinois. Other Nebraska towns were platted on

centers, is reviewed in a fine book that deserves to be better known: Glenn Chesney Quiett, *They Built the West: An Epic of Rails and Cities* (New York, 1934). While concentrating on the mining towns, two other studies provide material on Denver as well: Duane A. Smith, *Rocky Mountain Mining Camps: The Urban Frontier* (Bloomington, Ind., 1967); and Phyllis Flanders Dorset, *The New Eldorado: The Story of Colorado's Gold and Silver Rushes* (New York, 1970).

58. Louis L. Simonin, *The Rocky Mountain West in 1867* (Lincoln, Nebr., 1966), pp. 32–33. The accounts in this volume are assembled from a series of articles that Simonin wrote for the French periodical *Le Tour du Monde* in 1868. They are accompanied by many finely detailed engraved views of Denver and the Rocky Mountain mining towns.

59. As quoted in James C. Olson, *History of Nebraska* (Lincoln, Nebr., 1955), p. 84.

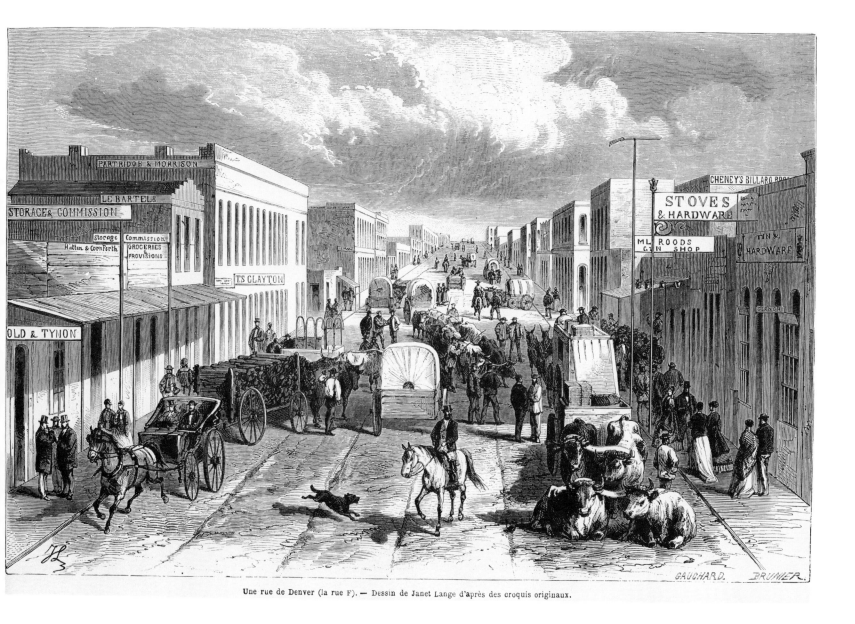

Une rue de Denver (la rue F). — Dessin de Janet Lange d'après des croquis originaux.

Figure 44. View of F Street (now 15th) in Denver, Colorado, 1867

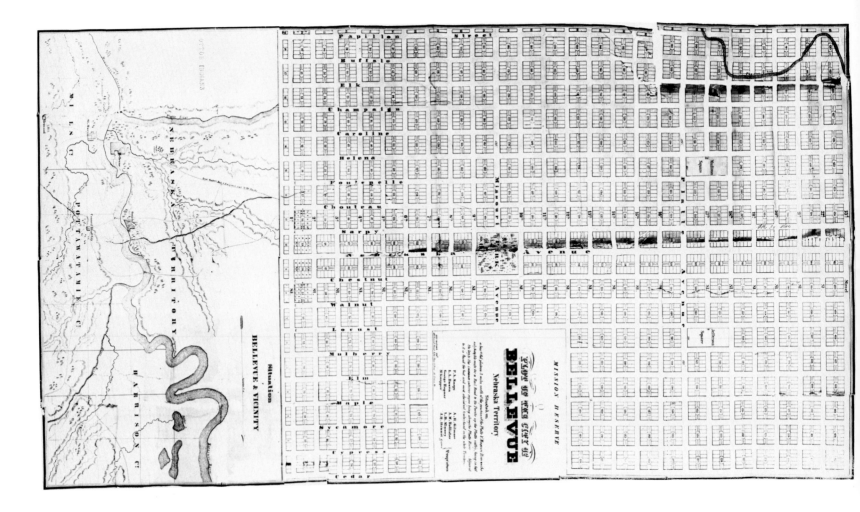

Figure 45. Bellevue, Nebraska, circa 1857

virgin sites, such as St. Deroin, Aspinwall, Nemaha City, Brownville (Figure 46), Peru, Nebraska City, Plattsmouth, Omaha, Tekamah, and Dakota City, to name only a few of the dozens of towns surveyed from 1854 to 1857 along the Nebraska shore of the Missouri River.[60]

For some of these towns, elaborate but hopelessly ambitious plans were devised. A colony of Roman Catholics from Iowa settled in St. John's City. In the plan for this city, three parks and a public square were set into the grid with some care (Figure 47). Streets leading to two of the parks entered at the middle of their sides, with the surrounding blocks being notched at the corners to provide the necessary space. North–south streets were conventionally numbered, but those running east–west constituted a partial hagiology of the canonized: St. Margaret, St. Elizabeth, St. Monica, St. Anastasia, and so forth. Even saints could not guarantee urban salvation, however, and after the financial panic of 1857 the town began a steady decline. By the mid-1870s it consisted of no more than a handful of houses, a fate shared by several others whose ghostly remains dotted the river bluffs.

The town company that platted Nebraska City in 1854 advertised its advantages and organized the usual auction of lots. A sardonic account of this event by a newspaper editor who served as auctioneer offers some amusing insights into the difficulties of frontier town promotion as well as into the inflated expectations of the proprietors:

> There must have been a multitude in attendance, which numbered at least seventeen or eighteen, and about five of them were not members of the town company, and against them every patriotic resident of this hopeful neighborhood . . . bid with great and vehement vigor. . . . It demonstrated the fact that there was some exchangeable value to lots. Everybody began to feel wealthy, and put on the comfortable airs of proprietary and pecuniary plethora. We had lots to sell; the whole world wanted to buy lots, and we could make a supply equal to demand, until the plains from the Missouri River to the Rocky Mountains had been chopped up into lots.[61]

Although Nebraska City's early years brought no great success, the town began to boom in 1858 when the large overland freighting firm of Russell, Majors, and Waddell announced that it was establishing its major depot at the city's western edge. Other firms similarly engaged in providing supply trains for towns and military posts in the West also came to Nebraska City, and until

60. A concise survey of this aspect of Nebraska's early settlement is Norman A. Graebner, "Nebraska's Missouri River Frontier, 1854–1860," *Nebraska History* 42 (December 1961): 213–35. For brief accounts of some of the towns that did not survive, see John C. Miller, "Ghost Towns in Otoe County," *Nebraska History* 18 (July–September 1937): 185–91. Much useful information about early towns is contained in J. Sterling Morton and Albert Watkins, *Illustrated History of Nebraska*, 3 vols. (Lincoln, Nebr., 1907–1913). A survey of some of the literature for this period is John Browning White, "Published Sources on Territorial Nebraska: An Essay and Bibliography," *Nebraska Historical Society Publications* 23 (1950).

61. J. Sterling Morton, as quoted from an unidentified source in A. T. Andreas, *History of the State of Nebraska* (Chicago, 1882), 3: 1201.

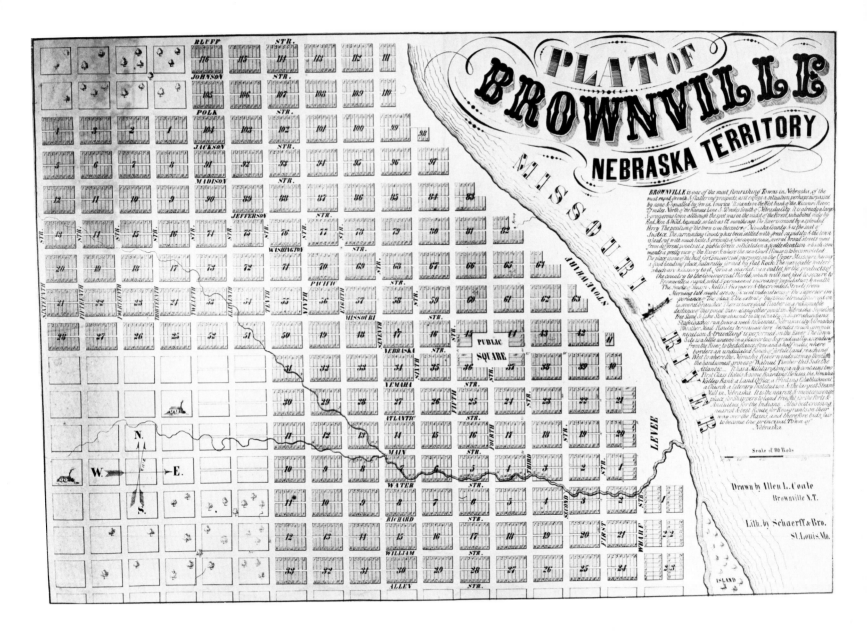

Figure 46. Brownville, Nebraska, circa 1855

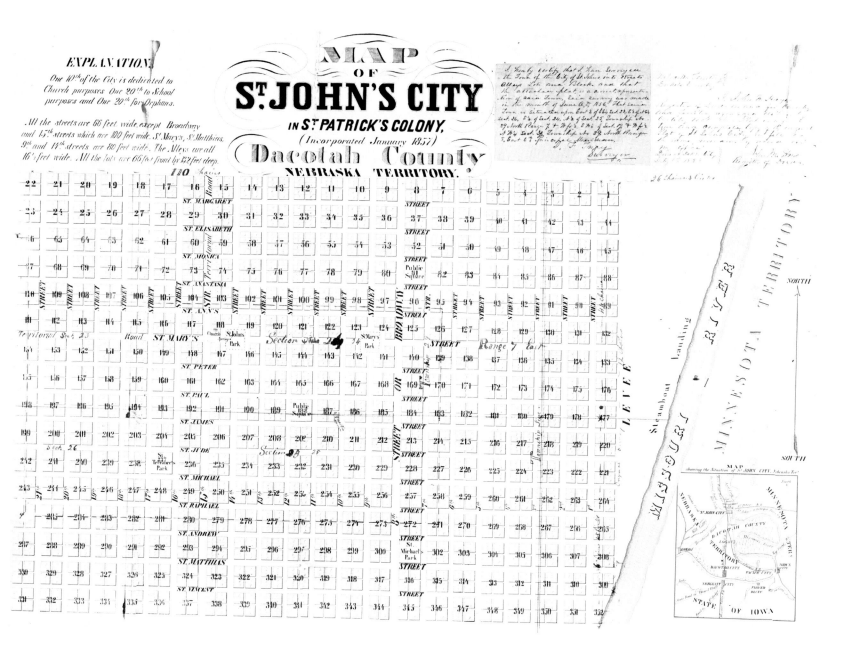

Figure 47. St. John's City, Nebraska, in 1856

the railroad ultimately replaced the wagon train, Nebraska City appeared destined to become a major metropolis. By 1856, however, when a frontier lithographer depicted the still thriving town (Figure 48), its greatest years lay behind it.[62]

Urban planning in early Kansas closely resembled that in Nebraska. Land speculators lined the Missouri River from the mouth of the Kansas River to the Nebraska border with dozens of hastily surveyed towns. Only twelve days after the territory was opened, a group from Weston, Missouri, laid out the town of Leavenworth three miles south of the fort by the same name (Figure 49). Like all the rest, the design of Leavenworth was based on a grid street system, but in addition to a public square of conventional size the plan called for an "Esplanade" along the river inserted between shallow waterfront blocks intended for warehouses.

Apparently Leavenworth was a successful speculation. That reliable observer of the West, Albert Richardson, noted that in 1857 "building lots . . . upon the river landing, were valued at ten thousand dollars. Three or four blocks back, they sold for two thousand, and on the hills half a mile away, for twelve hundred. Prices were fast rising, money plentiful, and everybody speculating."[63]

Leavenworth, Atchison, and many others among the twenty or so towns along the Missouri River were developed by pro-slavery groups. Countering this political element were Abolitionists, mostly from New England, who were responsible for creating several new towns to the west along the Kansas River.[64] The New England Emigrant Aid Company was organized for this purpose, to "dot Kansas with New England settlements" so that "New England principles and New England influences should pervade the whole Territory."[65]

Lawrence and Topeka, later to become the locations of the state university and the state capital, came into being as a result of the company's activities. A. D. Searle prepared the plan for Lawrence (Figure 50). He provided for grid streets eighty feet wide except for three major thoroughfares one hundred feet wide that connected groups of blocks reserved for parks, a college, and a number of other public or quasi-public uses. Searle thoughtfully reserved land for an industrial area, laid out smaller lots along the intended commercial street, and, around one cluster of four blocks designated for park use, varied

62. According to ibid., 3: 1203, in 1859 Russell, Major, and Waddell employed eleven hundred persons in Nebraska City, operated seven hundred wagons, and owned nearly six thousand yoke of oxen.

63. Albert D. Richardson, *Beyond the Mississippi* (Hartford, Conn., 1867), pp. 53–54. There is no better single contemporary source of information on Western town formation, speculative practices, and land frauds than this work by a skilled and respected journalist who lived for a time in Kansas and traveled extensively throughout the entire region.

64. For an account of the Abolitionist Missouri River town of Sumner, see Reps, *Cities of the American West*, pp. 439–41.

65. From a letter written by the organization's secretary in 1854, quoted in Edgar Langsdorf, "S. C. Pomeroy and the New England Emigrant Aid Company, 1854–1858," *Kansas Historical Quarterly* 7 (August 1938): 227–45.

Figure 48. Nebraska City, Nebraska, in 1868

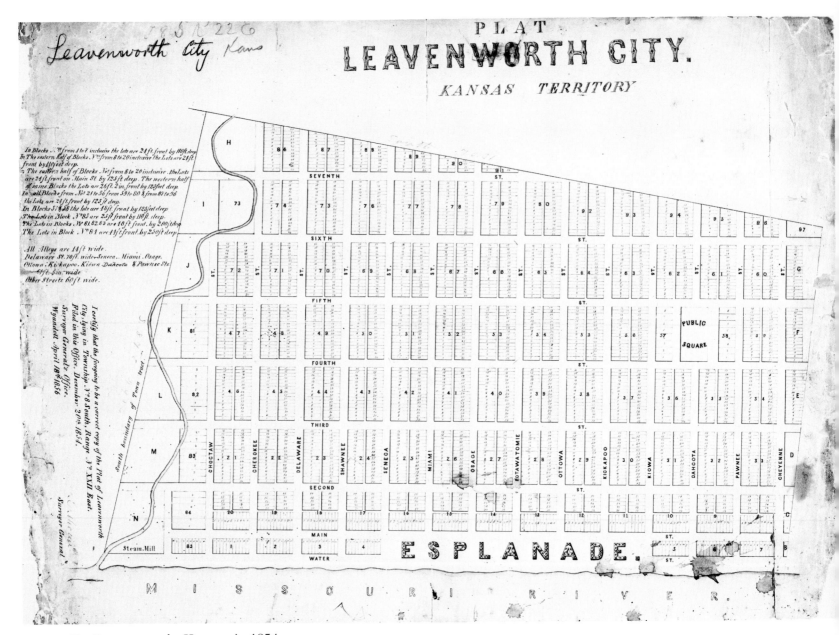

Figure 49. Leavenworth, Kansas, in 1854

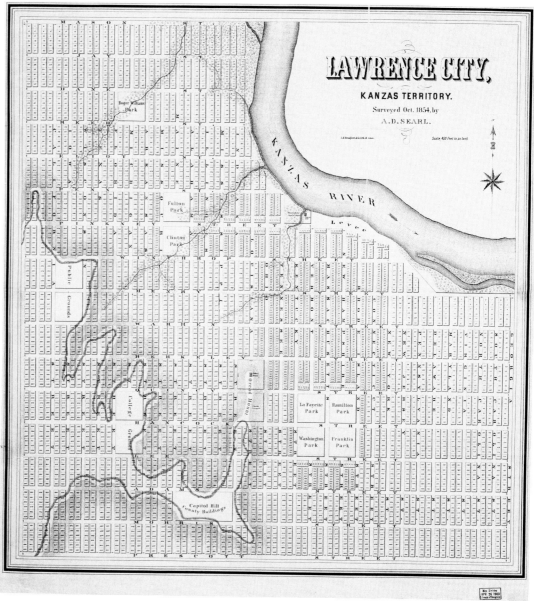

Figure 50. Lawrence, Kansas, in 1854

the orientation of the lots so that they fronted the open space. Rapid development of the new town was helped by the company's purchase of many prefabricated dwellings manufactured in Cincinnati.[66]

Searle also helped to plan Topeka, working with its founder, Cyrus K. Holliday, who came to Kansas to make a fortune in real estate. Holliday received aid from the New England Emigrant Aid Company in finding a suitable location and in recruiting New Englanders to settle at the chosen site well west of Lawrence on the Kansas River. Streets in widths of 80, 100, and 130 feet were oriented parallel and perpendicular to the course of the river, and inset in the grid were two tracts of twenty acres each that were reserved for public use (Figure 51). Holliday may have intended these large squares for the public buildings of the territorial capital.

Topeka eventually won the long and bitter fight to become the seat of government, and by 1866 construction had begun on the capitol, located on the easterly of the two large squares (Figure 52). That same year saw the arrival of the first trains of the Kansas Pacific Railroad, and two years later Topeka's founder, Cyrus Holliday, started construction of what was to become the Atchison, Topeka & Santa Fé line.[67]

Scores of other Kansas towns were planned in the period from 1854 to 1857, when the national financial panic put an end for a time to wholesale speculative townsite development. Not all of these towns survived—unfortunately, among those that didn't was the strikingly designed Council City (Figure 53) with its multiple civic squares—but pre-1860 maps of Kansas, like those of Nebraska to the north, document the almost incredible speed with which lasting urbanization occurred.

66. This early use of prefabrication and other aspects of the company's work at Lawrence are described in James C. Malin, "Emergency Housing at Lawrence, 1854," *Kansas Historical Society* 21 (Spring 1954): 34–49. Such structures were used in other Kansas settlements as well.

67. Topeka's founding, planning, and early development are dealt with in James L. King, *History of Shawnee County, Kansas* (Chicago, 1905); Wallace S. Baldinger, "The Amateur Plans a City," *Kansas Historical Quarterly* 12 (February 1943): 3–13; and F. W. Giles, *Thirty Years in Topeka (1886)* (Topeka, 1960).

TOWNS BY THE TRACKS

The long-delayed decision to build a transcontinental railroad began a new era of town planning. To the companies responsible for the construction of this railroad, Congress granted a right-of-way four hundred feet wide and alter-

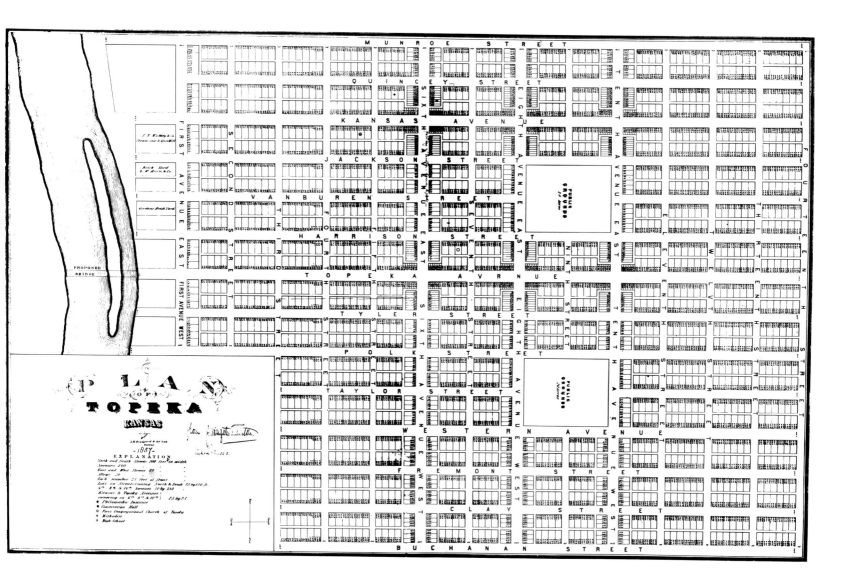

Figure 51. Topeka, Kansas, circa 1856

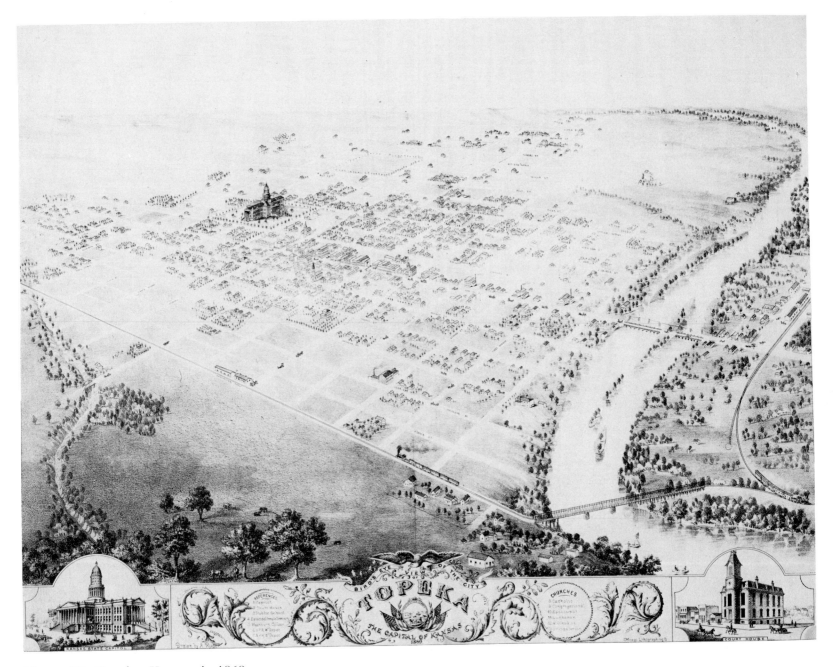

Figure 52. Topeka, Kansas, in 1869

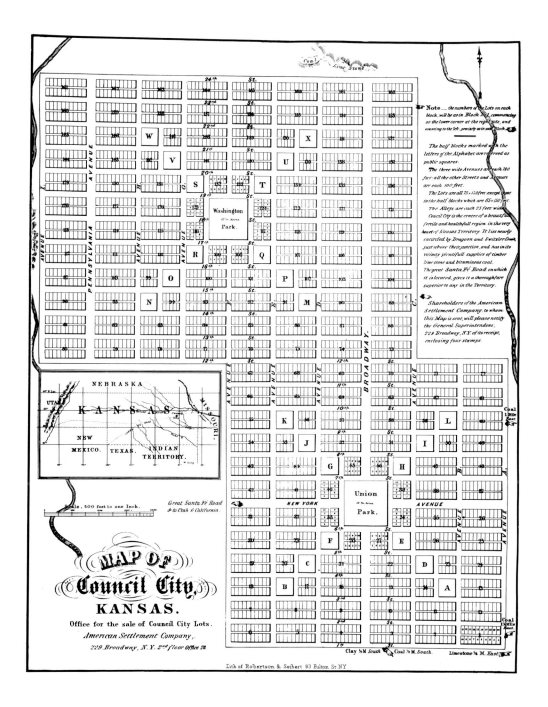

Figure 53. Council City, Kansas, circa 1855

nate square-mile sections of adjacent land. Generous federal loans were also made available. Similar terms were subsequently extended to several other lines.

Each Western railroad organized some kind of townsite subsidiary to plan and develop new communities on strategic sites selected from the railroads' land grants, and hundreds of communities resulted from their efforts. Virtually every town along such railroads as the Union Pacific, the Burlington, the Kansas Pacific, the Atchison, Topeka, & Santa Fé, the Northern Pacific, and the Great Northern was planned and promoted by engineers and land agents of the parent companies, as were most of the towns that developed along the many connecting lines that were laid as the Western rail network was extended.

Railroad-created towns usually began as end-of-track communities, planned to serve as temporary terminals before a new stretch of track beyond had been laid and rail service had been extended onward. William Bell, a young graduate of Cambridge University, found Salina, Kansas, on the Kansas Pacific line, to be anything but attractive when he visited it in 1867:

> On the open grass land . . . several broad streets could be seen, marked out with stakes, and crossing each other like a chessboard. . . . On each side of . . . [the] . . . main street were wooden houses, of all sizes and in all shapes of embryonic existence. Not a garden fence or tree was anywhere to be seen. . . . We found three billiard saloons, each with two tables, and the everlasting bar. Then came an ice-cream saloon, then a refreshment saloon. . . . All these "institutions," as well as a temporary school-house, and several small well-stocked shops . . . [were] . . . made of wood unpainted. . . . Trying to escape up a side street we discovered the Methodist Chapel, the Land Agency Office, labelled "Desirable town lot for sale," the Masonic Hall (temporary building), and the more pretentious foundations of the Free School, Baptist Chapel, and Episcopal Church. The suburbs consisted of tents of all shapes and forms, with wooden doors; shanties, half canvas, half wood. These were owned by squatters upon unsold lots.[68]

Bell was also struck by how many new towns of this kind could be seen and by how precarious their continued existence might be once their initial advantage of serving as terminals vanished. Observing the process of town founding along the Union Pacific, he noted that "town-making is reduced to a

68. William A. Bell, *New Tracks in North America* (London, 1869), 1: 19–20. Bell's two-volume record of his observations of Western railroad development is both accurate and entertaining.

69. Ibid., p. 18.

70. Many of Cheyenne's buildings, like those of other railroad towns, were prefabricated. A French mining engineer, visiting the city a year after its founding, was astounded to see houses arriving "by the hundreds from Chicago, already made, I was about to say, all furnished, in the style, dimensions, and arrangements you might wish. Houses are made to order in Chicago, as in Paris clothes are made to order at the Belle Jardiniere. Enter. Do you want a palace, a cottage, a city or country home; do you want it in Doric, Tuscan, or Corinthian; of one or two stories, an attic, Mansard gables? Here you are! At your service!" Simonin, *The Rocky Mountain West*, pp. 63–64.

system. The depot at the end of the line is only moved every two or three months; and . . . the town usually moves also, while nothing remains to mark the spot where thousands lived, but a station, a name, and a few acres of bare earth [Figure 54]. Last winter Cheyenne was the terminal depot . . . and increased in size to 5,000 inhabitants." He recalled a story told him by a friend who had watched a train pulling into Cheyenne, "laden with frame houses, boards, furniture, palings, old tents, and all the rubbish which makes up one of these mushroom 'cities.' The guard jumped off his van, and seeing some friends on the platform, called out with a flourish, 'Gentlemen, here's Julesburg.' The next train probably brought some other 'city' to lose for ever its identity in the great Cheyenne."[69]

Although Bell thus led his readers to believe that nothing remained after the railroad had built beyond these end-of-track communities, this is erroneous. Most of the towns managed to maintain at least some kind of existence; many of them recovered from the temporary loss of business and resumed their growth; and some, like Cheyenne, became important cities.

This Wyoming town was planned under the direction of Gen. Grenville Dodge, the chief engineer of the Union Pacific, as a division point where train crews were changed and locomotives and other rolling stock were serviced and repaired (Figure 55). All this generated sufficient employment to justify the construction of several hotels, stores, and other essential urban structures. Soon Cheyenne became a regional market center as well, with the development of farming and ranching in its hinterland (Figure 56). The generous grid of streets platted by the railroad land company began to fill with houses, churches, schools, public buildings, and other structures.[70]

Such places as Laramie and Benton, Wyoming; Reno, Nevada (Figure 57); and North Platte, Nebraska—to name but a few examples on the nation's first transcontinental line—were creatures of the railroad. Its surveyors and engineers established these towns well in advance of agricultural settlement, and they served successively as advance posts at the edge of the frontier, as a base for persons seeking farmsteads in the vicinity, and finally as stable communities well behind the zone of rapidly advancing settlement.

The Northern Pacific Railroad produced its own string of towns in Dakota Territory through the work of its townsite subsidiary, the Lake Superior and

"BUSTED!"—A DESERTED RAILROAD TOWN IN KANSAS.

Figure 54. A deserted railroad town in Kansas

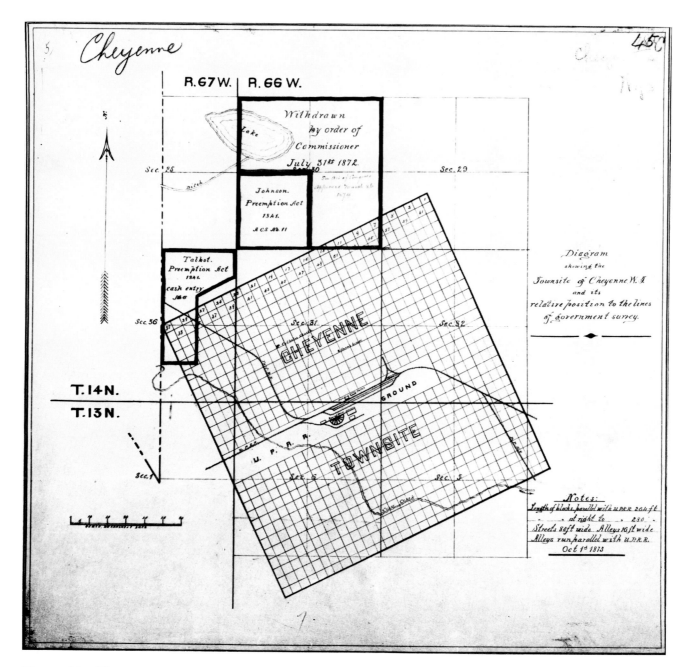

Figure 55. Cheyenne, Wyoming, in 1873, showing the townsite
planned in 1867 and its relationship to the federal land surveys

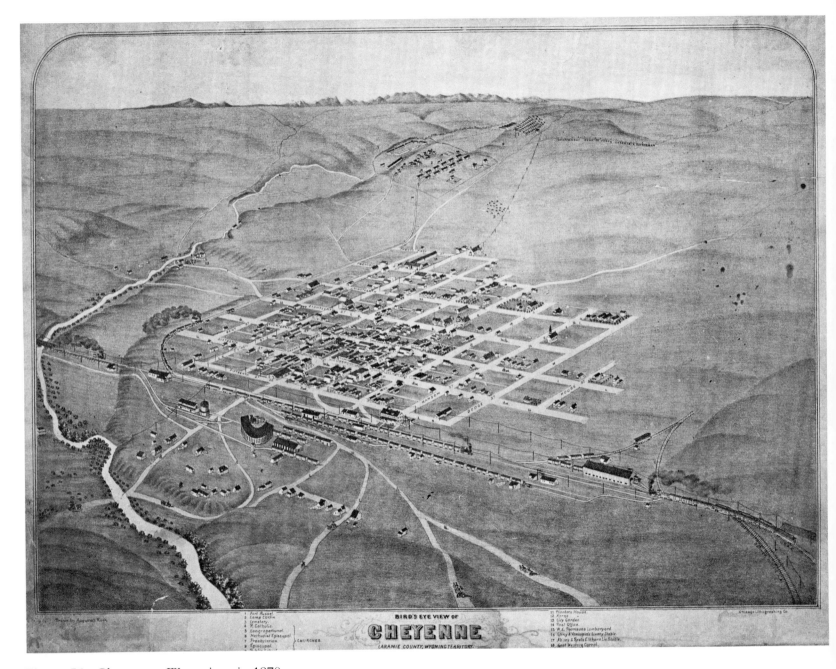

BIRD'S EYE VIEW OF
CHEYENNE
LARAMIE COUNTY, WYOMING TERRITORY.

Figure 56. Cheyenne, Wyoming, in 1870

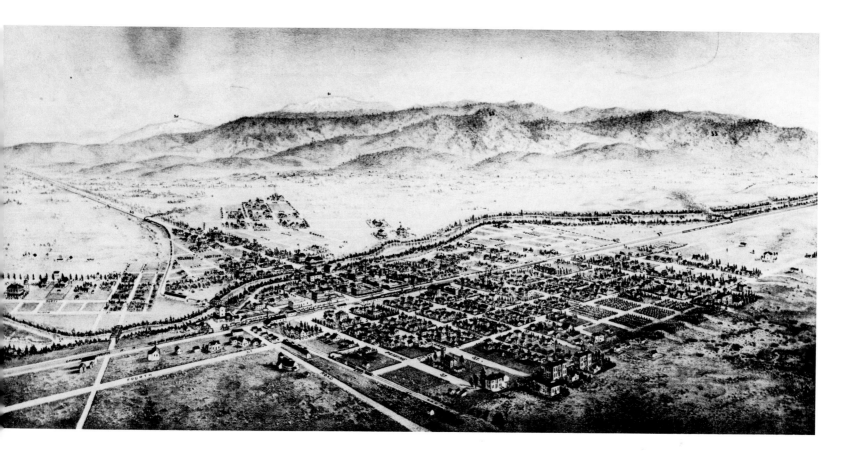

Figure 57. Reno, Nevada, in 1890

Puget Sound Company. Planned by the railroad in 1873 and named to attract German capital, Bismarck prospered as the supply center during the Black Hills mining boom and, later, as the territorial capital.

In 1883, after the Northern Pacific line had reached the Pacific Coast, the railroad's president, Henry Villard, brought former President Ulysses S. Grant to help preside over the ceremony of laying the cornerstone for the new capitol (Figure 58). The spectators at that event included such diverse characters as Lord James Bryce, whose thoughts on what he witnessed we will explore later, and Sitting Bull, evidently by that time forgiven for killing General Custer, who had been a frequent visitor in the town.[71]

Railroad townsite promotion was a profitable enterprise, perhaps in its initial years yielding revenues to the lines that were greater than those derived from passengers and freight, however mediocre or worse might have been the results in terms of urban planning. A publicist for the Northern Pacific, unusually candid in his words, summarized the techniques and revealed the results of the railroad's most important town in Montana:

> A few months ago . . . [Billings] . . . had no existence save in the brains of its inventors. The bare prairie was staked out in streets, avenues and parks. . . . A map was engraved, and within a few weeks after the place got its name, the "Billings boom" began to be talked of. . . . Billings lots were advertized in every town from St. Paul to Miles City, and whole blocks were sold in Chicago and New York. The purchasers knew no more about the valley of the Yellowstone than about that of the Congo. . . . Within sixty days from the time when Billings got a local habitation and a name, lots to the value of $202,000 were sold within its limits, and before thirty more days had elapsed the purchasers had advanced the imaginary value of their holdings from one hundred to three hundred per cent.[72]

Existing cities felt the impact of the railroad as well. Omaha boomed when it became apparent that it would serve as the eastern terminus of the Union Pacific, and land developers began to cut up the farmland surrounding the area first platted in 1854 when a townsite company had created one of Nebraska's first instant cities (Figure 59). That eccentric and enterprising frontier promoter, George Francis Train, bought five hundred acres at the city's outskirts, divided most of it into lots, invested in a hotel, and erected a large

71. In North Dakota, as in most Western territories and states, there had been a heated controversy over the location of the seat of government. In 1883 a commission was appointed to select the site for the capital. The law required the commission to meet for this purpose in Yankton, then the capital. Citizens of that town, claiming that only the governor and legislature had such power, prepared to serve writs on the members of the commission to prevent them from taking action. The commission chartered a special train, and as it passed slowly through Yankton passed the motion to approve Bismarck. Merle Potter, "The North Dakota Capital Fight," *North Dakota Historical Quarterly* 7 (October 1932): 25–53. For other studies of capital location fights, see Winkler, "Seat of Government of Texas"; Arthur S. Beardsley, "Early Efforts to Locate the Capital of Washington Territory," *Pacific Northwest Quarterly* 32 (July 1941): 239–87; Walter C. Winslow, "Contests over the Capital of Oregon," *Oregon Historical Society Quarterly* 9 (June 1908): 173–78; Morton and Watkins, *Illustrated History of Nebraska*, 1: 275–78, 298–302, 3: 8–24; Franklin G. Adams, "The Capitals of Kansas," *Kansas Historical Society Collections* 8 (1903–1904): 331–51; Eugene B. Chaffee, "The Political Clash between North and South Idaho over the Capital," *Pacific Northwest Quarterly* 29 (July 1938): 255–67; and Annie Laurie Bird, "A Footnote on the Capital Dispute in Idaho," *Pacific Northwest Quarterly* 36 (October 1945): 341–46, among others. Virtually every state history of the trans-Mississippi West deals with this issue, however briefly.

72. E. V. Smalley, "The New North-West," *Century Magazine* 24 (September 1882): 769–79. The early years of Billings are described in Waldo O. Kliewer, "The Foundations of Billings, Montana," *Pacific Northwest Quarterly* 31 (July 1940): 255–83.

VIEW OF THE CITY OF
BISMARCK, DAK.
CAPITAL OF DAKOTA
AND
COUNTY-SEAT OF BURLEIGH-COUNTY.
1883.

1 Capital Building.
2 High School Building.
3 Court House Building.
5 Dakota Block Building.
6 Union Block.
7 Raymond's Block.
8 Central Block.
9 First National Bank Building.
10 Mellon Brothers' Build'ng
11 Merchant's National Bank Building.
12 Flannery & Weatherby Building.
13 Temporary Capitol Building.
14 Sheridan House.
15 Merchant's Hotel.

16 Merchant's Hotel, Franklin House.
17 Banner House.
18 Pacific Hotel.
19 Western House.
20 Custer Hotel.
21 Montana Hotel.
22 Bismarck Daily Tribune,
23 Bismarck Daily Advertiser,
24 Dakota Daily Capital.
25 Planing Mill.
A Catholic Church.
B Episcopal Church.
C Presbyterian Church.
D Methodist Church.
E Baptist Church.

Figure 58. Bismarck, North Dakota, in 1883

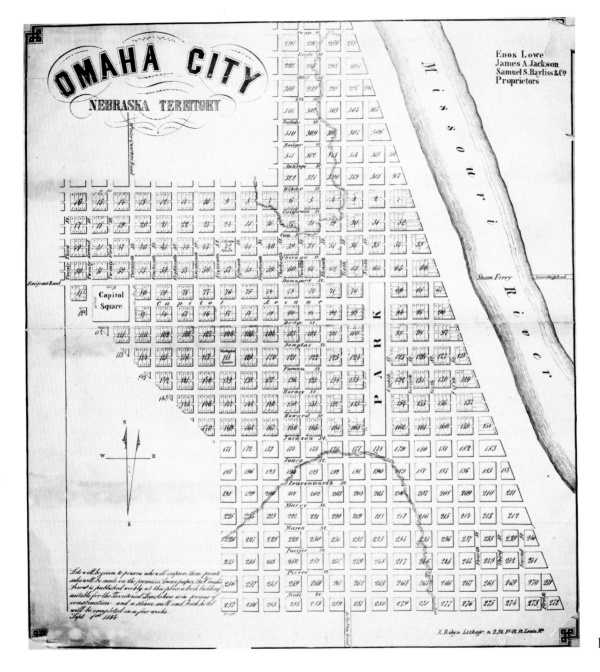

Figure 59. Omaha, Nebraska, in 1854

73. James W. Savage and John T. Bell, *History of the City of Omaha Nebraska* (New York, 1894), p. 101. Train's curious life is recounted in his *My Life in Many States and in Foreign Lands* (London, 1902).

74. Victor Westphall, "Albuquerque in the 1870's," *New Mexico Historical Review* 23 (October 1948): 253–68.

75. Las Vegas, New Mexico, began its existence as a tiny fortified *plaza* (or farm village) in 1833. This little municipality elected to pay a subsidy to the railroad to assure rail service. The Santa Fé line received a cash payment of ten thousand dollars, thirty acres of land for its depot and associated structures, and a half-interest in the four-hundred-acre addition platted as New Las Vegas. Westphall, "Albuquerque in the 1870's," p. 257. The effect of rail connections in Arizona and New Mexico is summarized in D. W. Meinig, *Southwest: Three Peoples in Geographical Change, 1600–1970* (New York, 1971), pp. 38–52. For Prescott, see Kitty Jo Parker Nelson, "Prescott: Sketch of a Frontier Capital, 1863–1900," *Arizoniana* 4 (Winter 1963): 17–26; and Pauline Henson, *Founding a Wilderness Capital: Prescott, A. T. 1864* (Flagstaff, Ariz., 1965). The development of Phoenix is described in James M. Barney, "Phoenix—A History of Its Pioneer Days and People," *Arizona Historical Review* 5 (January 1933): 264–68, and Frank C. Lockwood, *Pioneer Days in Arizona from the Spanish Occupation to Statehood* (New York, 1932). The plans of both Prescott and Phoenix are of interest. While both were gridiron designs, some care and thought were given to the location of public squares, and the straight streets and right-angled intersections were not entirely illogical for their flat sites. More extensive was the wildly ambitious plan in 1878 for Calabasas, near the southern border of Arizona. Occupying more than a square mile in the Santa Cruz River valley, it was intended by its

number of prefabricated dwellings that he had shipped from Chicago.[73] In 1868, when Omaha sat for its civic portrait, its residents were awaiting the completion of the Union Pacific with greedy excitement (Figure 60).

The railroad did not always bring prosperity. Most of the lines demanded "loans" or subsidies to enter an existing city in the pathway of construction. Not all towns responded favorably, and in many such cases the lines built rival towns that usually eclipsed the older settlements nearby. One example was Albuquerque, a long-established community of Spanish origins, dating from 1706. Residents of the town opposed the railroad's plans to slash its lines across valuable irrigated farm fields. The line responded by acquiring a large site two miles to the east and planning New Albuquerque (Figure 61). Shortly thereafter, most of the businesses and many of the citizens of the old town moved to the new location with its better transportation facilities.[74]

In other places in the Southwest the long-awaited railroad stepped up the tempo of urban growth. At Las Vegas, New Mexico, a major addition to the sleepy little trading center provided housing and business sites for a burgeoning population attracted by real estate opportunities opened up by the Santa Fé line (Figure 62). Prescott, on the other hand, planned with ample public sites in 1864 as the capital of Arizona Territory, did not obtain rail service until 1893 by a branch line to the Santa Fé (Figure 63). It was too late by four years, for in 1889 the legislature had transferred the seat of government to Phoenix. That town, laid out in 1870 by three townsite commissioners elected by residents wishing to settle in the vicinity, also was bypassed by the nearest transcontinental line, the Southern Pacific (Figure 64). Enterprising landowners and merchants furnished the capital to build their own line—the Maricopa and Phoenix—to achieve the rail service necessary for survival and prosperity in the competition for Western urban supremacy.[75]

Nowhere was railroad-related town planning and promotion pursued so avidly as in and around Los Angeles when the city was first linked to the rest of the country in 1876 via connections at San Francisco. Until that time Los Angeles had been growing on the orderly, if rather unimaginative, plans prepared for its expansion by Lt. Edward Ord in 1849 and by Henry Hancock in 1853 (Figure 65). Ord, at the request of the city council, extended the old Spanish pueblo plan by adding two grid additions to the north and south.

Figure 60. Omaha, Nebraska, in 1868

Figure 61. Albuquerque, New Mexico, in 1886

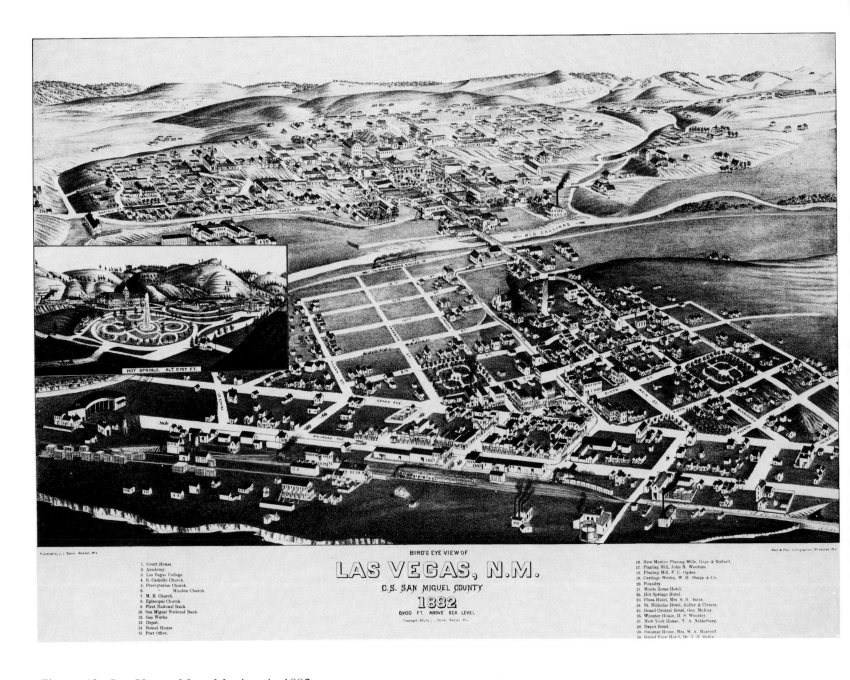

BIRD'S EYE VIEW OF

LAS VEGAS, N.M.

C.S. SAN MIGUEL COUNTY

1882

6400 FT. ABOVE SEA LEVEL

Copyright 1882 by J. J. Stoner, Madison, Wis.

1. Court House.
2. Academy.
3. Las Vegas College.
4. R. Catholic Church.
5. Presbyterian Church.
   Mission Church.
6. M. E. Church.
7. Episcopal Church.
8. First National Bank.
9. First National Bank.
10. San Miguel National Bank
11. Gas Works.
12. Depot.
13. Round House.
14. Post Office.

16. New Mexico Planing Mills, Hope & Bullard.
17. Planing Mill, John B. Wootten.
18. Planing Mill, P. C. Ogden.
19. Carriage Works, W. H. Shupp & Co.
20. Foundry.
21. Monte Xmas Hotel.
22. Hot Springs Hotel.
23. Plaza Hotel, Mrs. S. B. Davis.
24. St. Nicholas Hotel, Keller & Clema.
25. Grand Central Hotel, Geo. McKay.
26. Wooster House, H. S. Wooster.
27. New York House, T. A. Netterberg.
28. Depot Hotel.
29. Summer House, Mrs. M. A. Maxwell.
30. Grand View Hotel, Dr. J. H. Sutfin.

Figure 62. Las Vegas, New Mexico, in 1882

Figure 63. Prescott, Arizona, in 1864

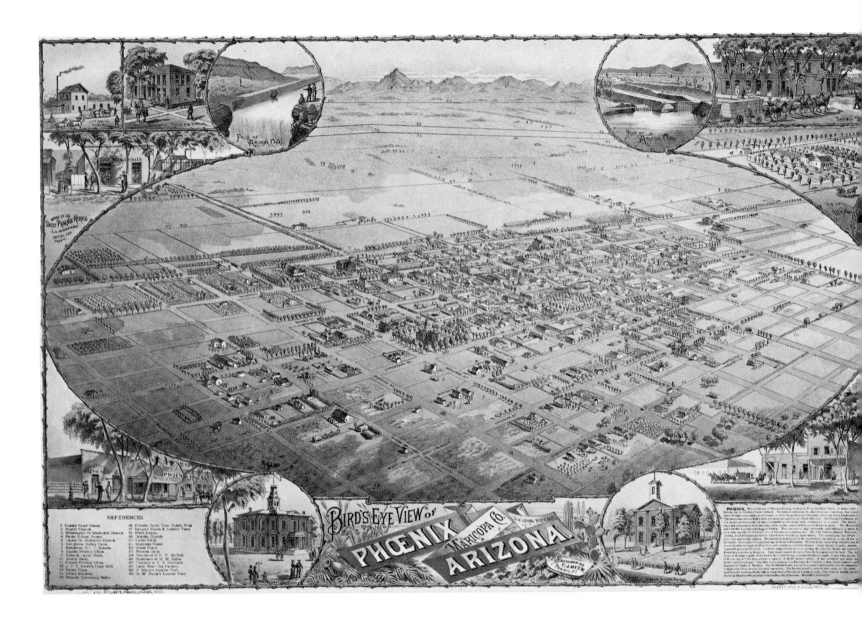

Figure 64. Phoenix, Arizona, in 1885

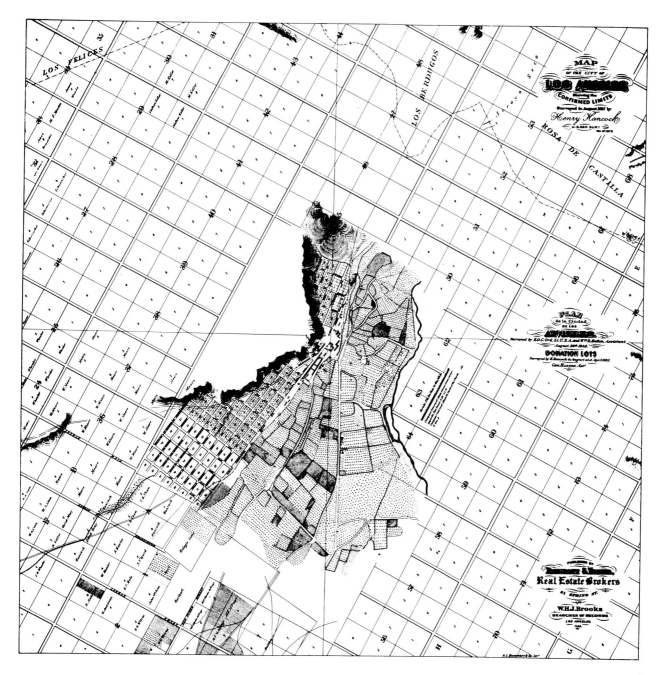

Figure 65. Los Angeles, California, and the additions planned
in 1849 and 1853 by Edward Ord and Henry Hancock

Hancock's contribution was a division of the large remaining portion of the twenty-eight-square-mile pueblo grant into a super-gridiron of wide streets forming large blocks made up of thirty-five-acre parcels.[76]

Prior to 1870, however, most of the town's buildings could be found near the plaza, along the early streets leading from it, and on the more centrally located blocks of the two grid extensions planned by Ord (Figure 66). At the end of its first decade under the American flag, the city's appearance had scarcely changed, until the prospect of rail connections to the outside world aroused its property owners to new possibilities.

They began to subdivide Hancock's rectangular tracts or other holdings that had passed into private ownership before the Hancock survey. East Los Angeles and Brooklyn Heights thus made their appearance in the 1870s as two of the earliest suburbs of the now booming city (Figure 67). Many completely new towns were also planned within the orbit of Los Angeles, Santa Monica among them (Figure 68). And in the vicinity of the several old Spanish missions of the region extensive additions were laid out to provide accommodations for the rapidly increasing population. In this manner, such communities as San Gabriel, San Luis Obispo, and Ventura began their modern development.[77] Except for Brooklyn Heights, with its curving streets that imitated the Olmstedian manner then so fashionable in the East, all of these additions, new towns, and expansion projects used some variety of the grid system.

This first Southern California land boom came to a sudden but temporary end with the national depression of the late 1870s, but the arrival of the Santa Fé Railroad in the mid-1880s fanned the flames of speculation to new intensity. Eastern land speculators hastened to the region, coming, as one observer noted, "not to build up the country, but to make money, honestly if they could not make it any other way. It is needless to say they made it the other way."[78] An orgy of town planning resulted.

In January 1886, real estate sales in the county of Los Angeles exceeded $1 million. By the end of the year monthly sales averaged three times that amount, and in July 1887 sales reached nearly $12 million.[79] Freshly subdivided land in the city and lots in new suburban towns accounted for the bulk of these transactions (Figure 69). Along the line of the Santa Fé thirteen

promoter to become the chief point of entry for trade with Mexico. An elaborate hotel was constructed, but the venture proved a failure, and by the end of the century the town had only a handful of buildings. For views of the Calabasas hotel and other early views of Arizona towns and buildings, see James E. Sherman and Barbara H. Sherman, *Ghost Towns of Arizona* (Norman, Okla., 1969), and Andrew Wallace, *The Image of Arizona: Pictures from the Past* (Albuquerque, N.M., 1971). A reproduction of the Calabasas plan can be found in Reps, *Cities of the American West*, fig. 18.26, p. 629.

76. J. M. Guinn, "From Pueblo to Ciudad: The Municipal and Territorial Expansion of Los Angeles," *Historical Society of Southern California Publications* 7 (1908): 216–21; "The Plan of Old Los Angeles and the Story of Its Highways and Byways," *Historical Society of Southern California Publications* 3 (1895): 40–50; and W. W. Robinson, "Story of Ord's Survey as Disclosed by the Los Angeles Archives," *Historical Society of Southern California Quarterly* 19 (September–December 1937): 121–31.

77. The best study of Southern California's urban growth in the 1870s and 1880s under speculative influence is Glenn S. Dumke, *The Boom of the Eighties in Southern California* (San Marino, Calif., 1963).

78. J. M. Guinn, "The Great Real Estate Boom of 1887," *Historical Society of Southern California Publications* 1 (1890): 13–21.

79. Dumke, *The Boom of the Eighties*, p. 46–49.

Figure 66. Los Angeles, California, in 1857

Figure 67. Los Angeles, California, in 1877

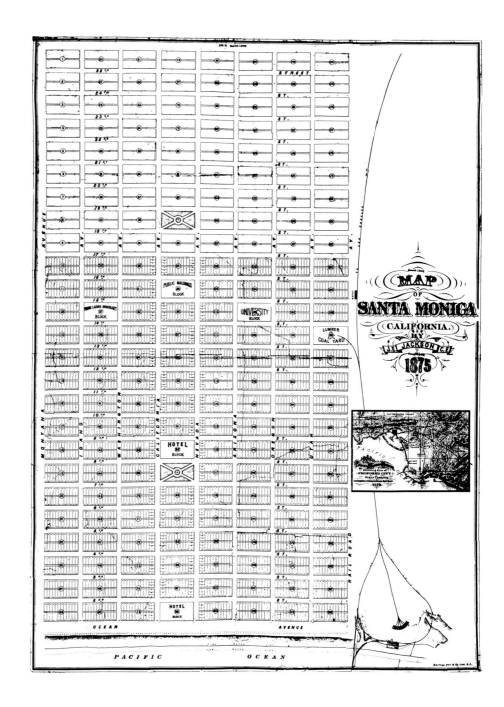

Figure 68. Santa Monica, California, in 1875

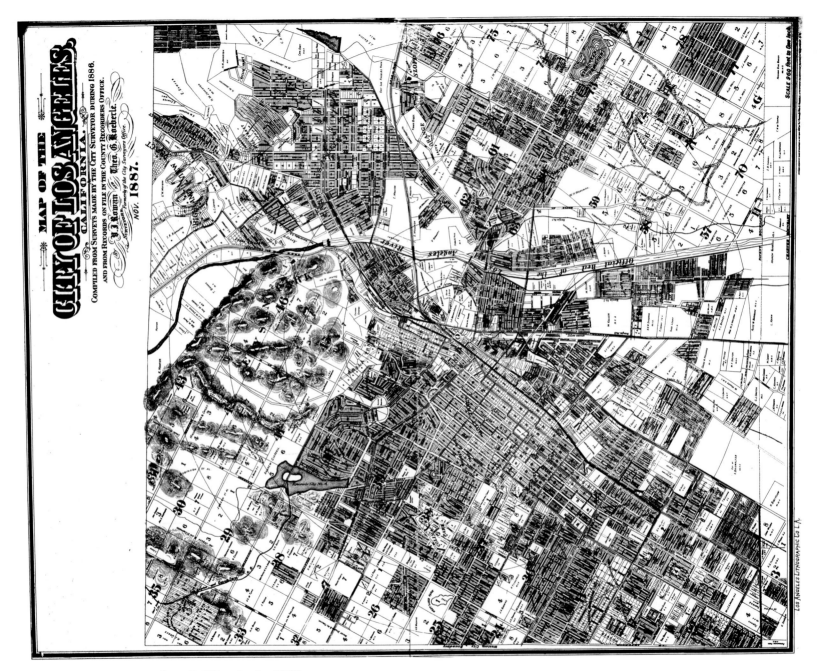

Figure 69. Los Angeles, California, in 1887

80. Guinn, "Real Estate Boom," p. 15.

81. For the work of Davis, see Andrew F. Rolle, "William Heath Davis and the Founding of American San Diego," *California Historical Society Quarterly* 31 (March 1952): 33–48; for Horton, consult Theodore S. Van Dyke, *The City and County of San Diego* (San Diego, 1888), pp. 21–28. It is to Horton that San Diego may owe its superb Balboa Park, for it was he who suggested that its 1,440 acres be reserved for this purpose from the remaining lands of the original pueblo grant. His many activities in urban planning and development have gone unrecognized outside of his adopted city. See Elizabeth C. MacPhail, *The Story of New San Diego and of Its Founder, Alonzo E. Horton* (San Diego, 1969).

townsites were platted during three months in the spring of 1887. By the end of the year, between Los Angeles and San Bernardino County, "a distance of thirty-six miles . . . there were twenty-five cities and towns, an average of one to each mile and a half of the road." Nearby, along the rival Southern Pacific, eight more towns had been surveyed, with three others in the territory between the two rights-of-way.[80]

Some developers used exotic plans in efforts to make their speculative towns stand out as distinctive. Cahuenga had an elaborately designed combination of grid, circular, and winding streets. Corona boasted of a circular street one mile in diameter enclosing a more conventional grid. Redondo Beach also was given an intricate pattern, with radial and gently curving streets slashing across others of a modified orthogonal system (Figure 70). Most, however, depended on the promotional efforts of their sponsors rather than on unusual designs to compete in the marketplace for urban lots: Hollywood, Monrovia, Chicago Park, Azusa, Glendora, Altamont, and countless others.

In the process Los Angeles was transformed from a small city to the beginnings of a modern metropolis. A view published in 1891 shows the community on the threshold of a new period of expansion, for the inevitable depression following the great land boom could not check the city's growth for long (Figure 71). Here and at such places as Pasadena, frenzied speculation and empty promises were mixed with solid achievement in urban development as most of those lured from the East to dabble in land sales and town lots settled down to more productive occupations.

Townsite promoters in and around San Diego also eagerly participated in the Southern California land boom. As in Los Angeles, San Diego's municipal council in 1849 arranged for a survey of the entire Spanish pueblo grant and in the process had its engineer lay out new streets adjoining the old town as well as a projected port community on the coast (Figure 72). Later, two energetic speculators, William Heath Davis and Alonzo Erastus Horton, bought enormous tracts of land from the municipality at bargain prices and planned additional towns nearby.[81] New San Diego (Figure 73) and the even larger Horton Addition (Figure 74) thus added to the supply of building sites.

Most of the thousands of lots went unsold until the Santa Fé Railroad pro-

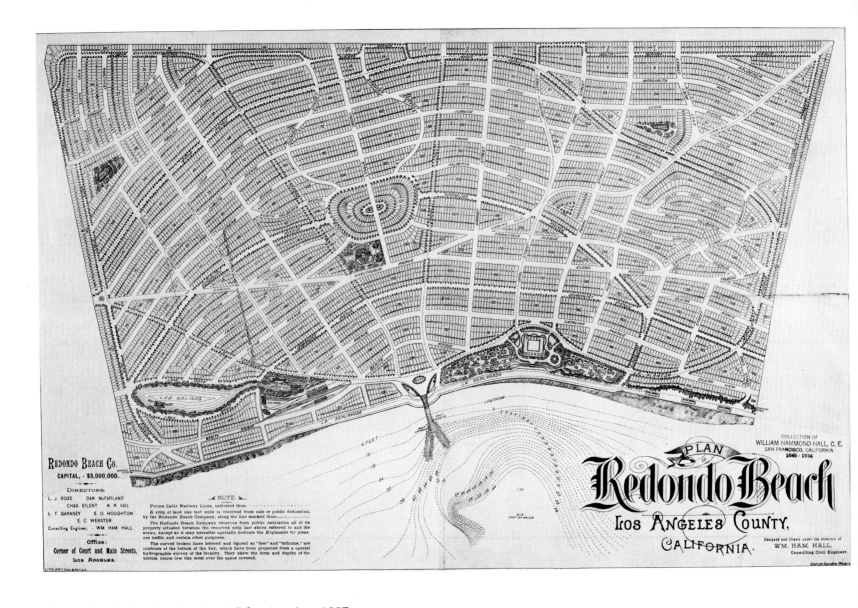

Figure 70. Redondo Beach, California, circa 1887

Figure 71. Los Angeles, California, in 1891

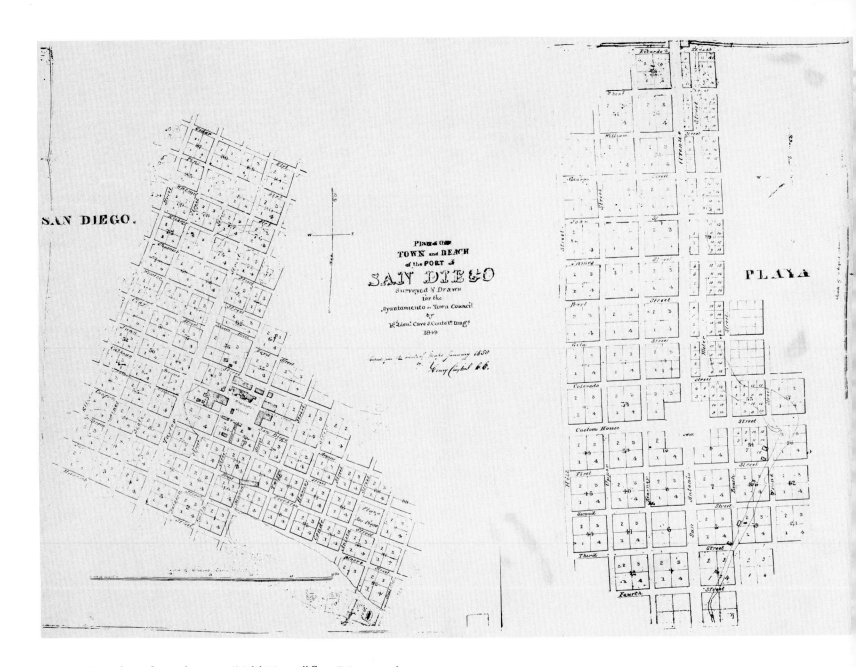

Figure 72. Plans for enlarging "Old Town" San Diego and for the new town of La Playa on San Diego Bay in 1849

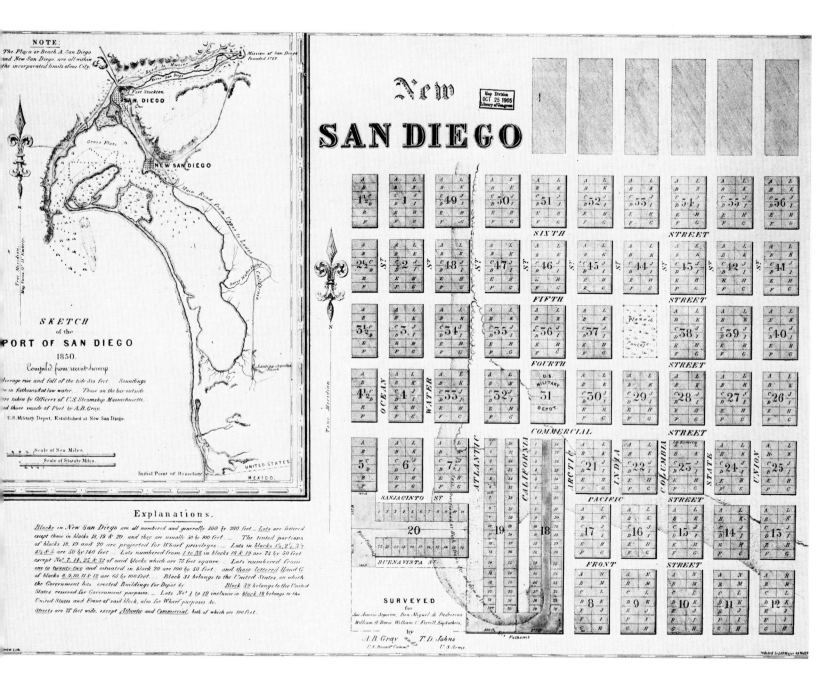

Figure 73. New San Diego, California, in 1850

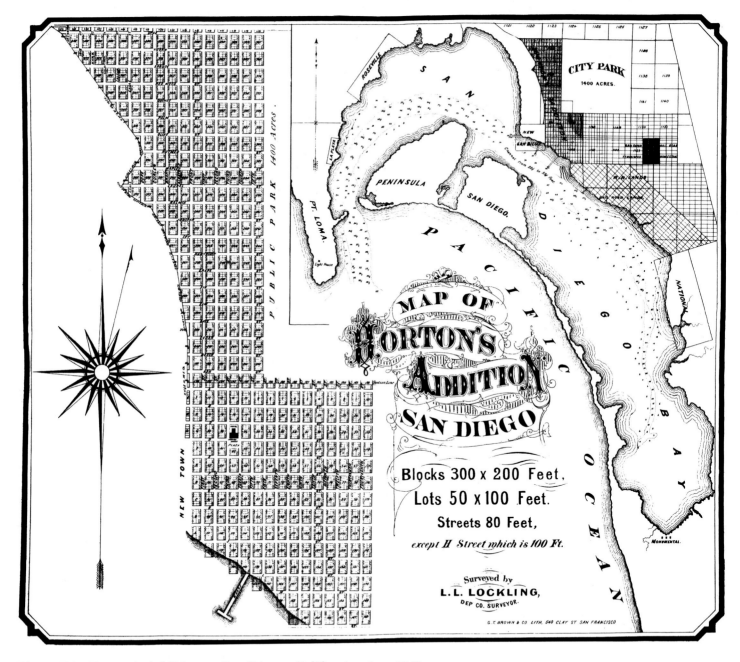

Figure 74. Horton's Addition to San Diego, California, circa 1868

vided San Diego with direct connections to the East in the mid-1880s. As the tracks approached, a frenzy of land speculation gripped the city. Prices shot up, with many business lots jumping from twenty-five dollars a front foot to an astounding twenty-five hundred dollars. Buying mostly on credit, newcomers from the East began to fill the voids on the several grid systems that earlier speculators had left for them to occupy (Figure 75).

At least one new town, Chula Vista, was created by the Santa Fé itself; individual speculators were responsible for most of the rest, including Otay, Oceanside, Encinitas, Sorrento, La Jolla, Pacific Beach, and Ocean Beach on the coast and Escondido, Lakeside, and La Mesa among the dozens of inland communities. The most interesting plan of all was that for Coronado Beach, across the bay from San Diego (Figure 76). Here the designers in 1884 managed to combine all three major patterns, grid, radial, and curvilinear, as an elaborate and fascinating background for the large and luxurious Hotel Coronado.[82]

In the northern part of California the influence of the railroad was less marked although far from unimportant. San Francisco's basic pattern had been established long before the driving of the Golden Spike in 1869 signaled to a waiting nation that the two parts of the country had been linked by iron rails. Shortly after American occupation of California in 1846, the military commander of San Francisco retained Jasper O'Farrell to resurvey and extend the town, a project completed early in 1847 when the surveyor revealed his grid design that rectified the confusing acute angles of Vioget's plan (Figure 77).

As population increased, additional lots were needed, and city officials set O'Farrell to work again. He extended some of the street lines of his earlier grid into the water to create more building sites and added several blocks on the remaining sides of the town to the north, west, and south. Beyond the southern extension of his first grid he laid out a second grid system at a forty-five-degree angle to the first, dividing the two areas by Market Street, 110 feet wide.

Another extension in 1849 by William Eddy, then city surveyor, enlarged San Francisco still further (Figure 78). The two planners managed to reserve only four open spaces. One, Portsmouth Square, had its beginning in Vioget's

82. The growth of San Diego and the speculative planning of the towns in this area during the late-nineteenth-century land booms are described in Reps, *Cities of the American West*, pp. 239–45, 276–81.

Drawn by E. S. Glover and Published by Schneider & Kueppers, San Diego.

Entered according to Act of Congress, in the year 1876, by Schneider & Kueppers, in the Office of the Librarian of Congress, at Washington, D. C.

A. L. Bancroft & Co., Lithographers, San Francisco, Cal.

Showing the central portion of the city, with the *actual* improvements; San Diego Bay and Peninsula, the Entrance to the Harbor, Point Loma, and the Los Coronados Islands, twenty miles distant in the Pacific Ocean.

The County Seat of San Diego County and the proposed Terminus of the Texas Pacific Railroad. Present Population, about 3,000. A commercial town; publishes two newspapers, "San Diego Union" and "World," weekly and daily editions.

BIRD'S EYE VIEW OF
SAN DIEGO, CALIFORNIA
1876
FROM THE NORTH-EAST, LOOKING SOUTH-WEST.

1. Presbyterian Church.	5. Catholic Church.	9. Bank of San Diego.
2. Baptist Church.	6. Public Schools.	10. Commercial Bank.
3. Methodist Church.	7. Point Loma Seminary.	11. City Hall.
4. Episcopal Church.	8. San Diego Academy.	12. Central Market Building.

13. Horton's Hall.	17. Lyon House.	21. Book Store of Schneider & Kueppers.
14. Telegraph Offices.	18. Bay View Hotel.	22. San Diego Foundry.
15. Horton House.	19. Government Barracks.	23. San Diego Planing Mill.
16. San Diego County Court House.	20. San Diego Planing Mill.	24. City Brewery.

Figure 75. San Diego, California, in 1876

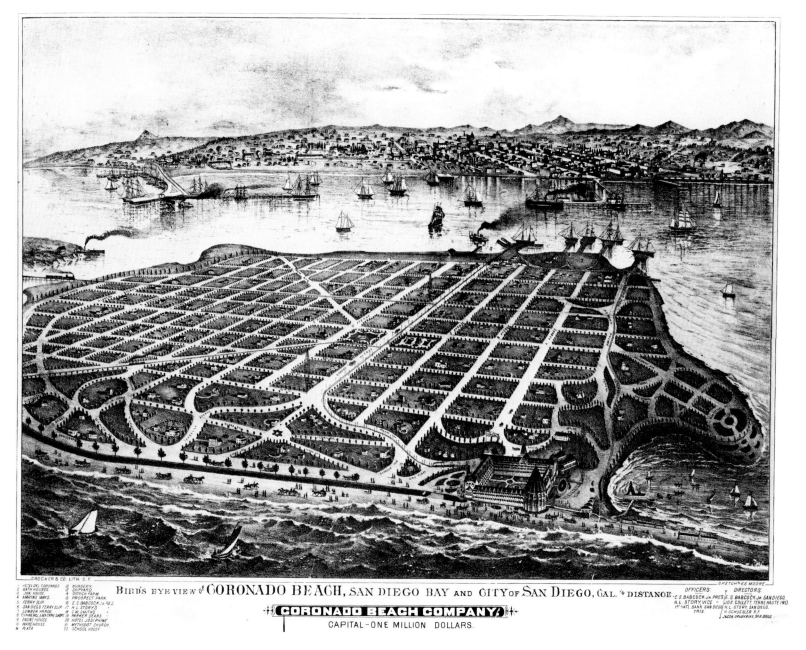

BIRD'S EYE VIEW OF CORONADO BEACH, SAN DIEGO BAY AND CITY OF SAN DIEGO, CAL. ⅘ DISTANCE

CRACKER & CO. LITH. S.F.

SKETCH BY E.S. MOORE

1 HOTEL DEL CORONADO.
2 BATH HOUSES.
3 JOK. HOUSE.
4 MARINE WAYS.
5 FERRY SLIP.
6 SAN DIEGO FERRY SLIP.
7 LUMBER YARD.
8 PLANING MILL & MACHINE SHOP.
9 ENGINE HOUSE.
10 WAREHOUSE.
N PLAZA.

12 NURSERY.
13 SHIPYARD.
14 OSTRICH FARM.
15 PROSPECT PARK.
16 E.S. BABCOCK JR RES.
17 H.L. STORY'S
18 C.W. SMITH'S
19 PARKER DEARS
20 HOTEL JOSIPHINE
21 METHODIST CHURCH
22 SCHOOL HOUSE.

CORONADO BEACH COMPANY
CAPITAL—ONE MILLION DOLLARS.

OFFICERS
E.S. BABCOCK Jr. PRES.
H.L. STORY VICE
1ST NATL. BANK, SAN DIEGO
TRES.

DIRECTORS
E.S. BABCOCK JR SAN DIEGO.
JOS. COLLETT TERRE HAUTE IND.
H.L. STORY, SAN DIEGO.
H. SCHUSSLER, S.F.
JACOB GRUENDIKE, SAN DIEGO.

Figure 76. Coronado, California, circa 1887

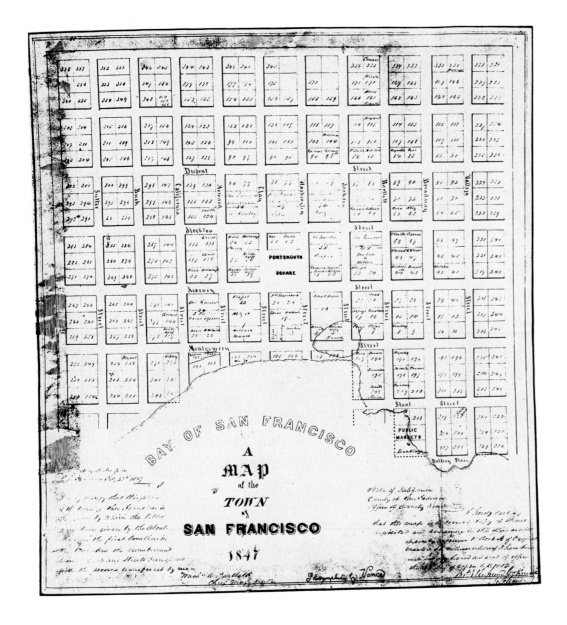

Figure 77. Jasper O'Farrell's plan for San Francisco, California, in 1847

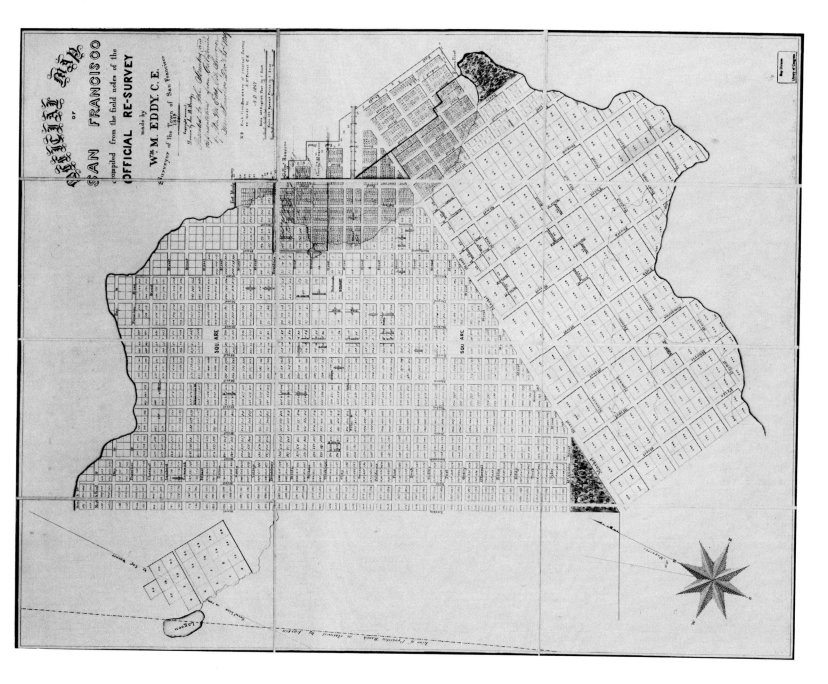

Figure 78. San Francisco, California, in 1849, as extended by Jasper O'Farrell and William Eddy

plan and was enlarged by O'Farrell. Eddy laid out a small square south of Market Street. Two others, planned by O'Farrell, became important civic spaces: Washington Square and the far more impressive Union Square in the heart of the modern city's shopping district.

With these trifling exceptions, the rapidly growing city had no parks or other open spaces until 1856 when a large new addition was planned during the administration of Mayor James Van Ness (Figure 79). Perhaps the mechanically located squares in this Western Addition represented an unimaginative response to a stinging criticism published a year earlier. The authors of this article rebuked city officials for the lack of parks, attributing this "to the jealous avarice of the city projectors in turning every square . . . [yard] . . . of the site, to an available building lot."

As to the dull and pervasive grid, they complained that "the eye is wearied and the imagination quite stupefied, in looking over the numberless square—all square—building blocks, and mathematically straight lines of streets, miles long and every one crossing a host of others at right angles, stretching over sandy hill, chasm and plain, without the least regard to the natural inequalities of the ground. Not only is there no public park or garden, but there is not even a circus, oval, open terrace, broad avenue or any ornamental line of street or building." [83]

By 1868, the year before California and the East were linked by the railroad, San Francisco thus had received its basic urban pattern formed by a series of grids stamped across its steep hills as if the site had stood somewhere on the plains of Kansas or Nebraska (Figure 80). City officials were responsible for virtually all of what had been done, for they proceeded, as did their counterparts in Los Angeles, with the powers of public landownership that they had inherited from the Mexican era in the form of the standard Hispanic pueblo grant. [84]

The railroad further enhanced San Francisco's supremacy as the greatest city of the West. In the general climate of economic optimism, expansion, and speculation, the railroad also stimulated the growth of San José (Figure 81), Monterey, and Santa Cruz, although the results were not so dramatic. Down the peninsula from San Francisco a series of attractive residential communities emerged: Menlo Park, Redwood City, San Mateo, and Burlingame, among

83. Frank Soulé, John H. Givon, and James Nisbet, *The Annals of San Francisco (1855)* (Palo Alto, Calif., 1966), p. 160. For other early criticisms of San Francisco's plan, see M. G. Upton, "The Plan of San Francisco," *Overland Monthly* 2 (February 1869): 131–37, and Samuel Bowles, *Across the Continent . . . in the Summer of 1865* (Springfield, Mass., 1869), pp. 288–90.

84. Two of the many books on San Francisco are especially helpful in tracing the planning and development of that city. See Mel Scott, *The San Francisco Bay Area: A Metropolis in Perspective* (Berkeley, 1959), and Roger W. Lotchin, *San Francisco, 1846–1856: From Hamlet to City* (New York, 1974). Barth's *Instant Cities* has already been noted. See also B. S. Brooks, "Alcalde Grants in the City of San Francisco," *Pioneer, or California Monthly Magazine* 1 (April 1854): 193–200; Bruno Fritzsche, "San Francisco, 1845–1848: The Coming of the Land Speculator," *California Historical Quarterly* 51 (Spring 1972): 17–34; and Helen Putnam Van Sicklen, "Jasper O'Farrell: His Survey of San Francisco," *Quarterly of the Society of California Pioneers* 10 (1933): 85–100.

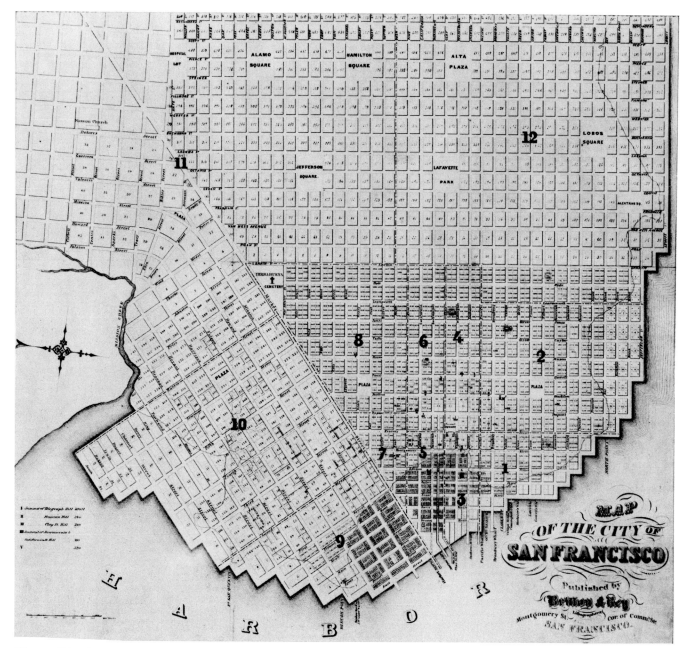

Figure 79. San Francisco, California, circa 1856, with the Western Addition planned during the Van Ness administration

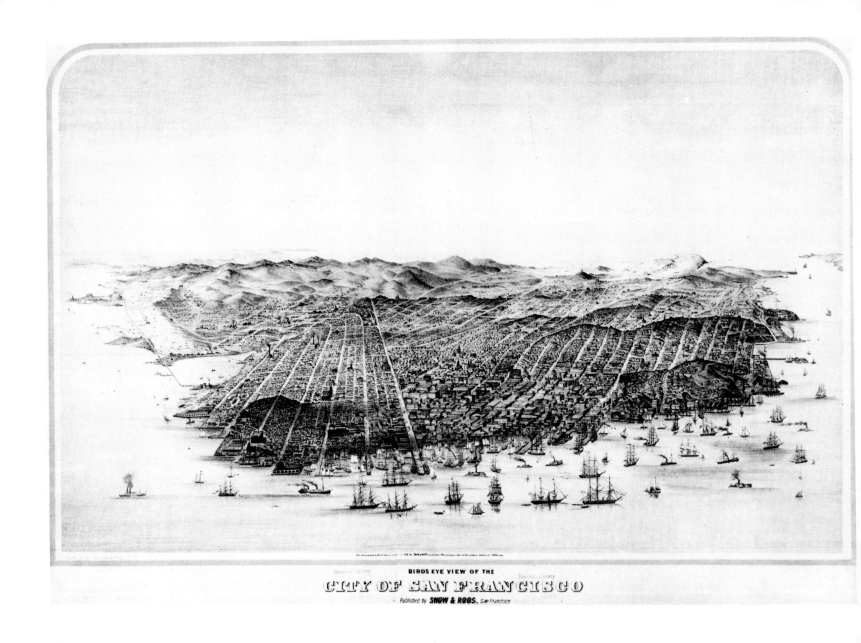

BIRDS EYE VIEW OF THE
CITY OF SAN FRANCISCO
Published by SNOW & ROOS., San Francisco

Figure 80. San Francisco, California, in 1868

CITY OF SAN JOSE, CAL. 1875.

PUBLISHED BY W.C.GIFFORD

Figure 81. San José, California, in 1875

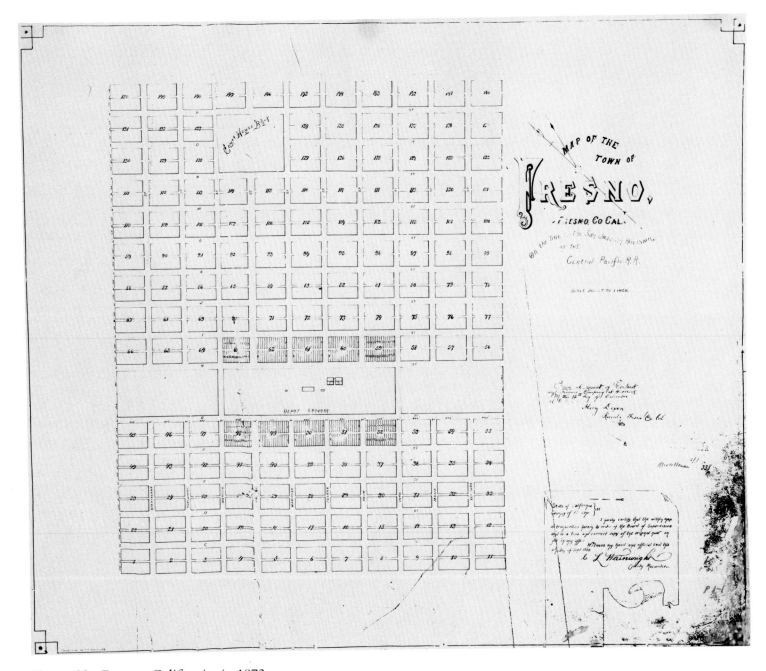

Figure 82. Fresno, California, in 1873

85. Economic development and population growth as a result of the railroad were viewed with some reserve by Henry George. See his "What the Railroad Will Bring Us," *The Overland Monthly* 1 (October 1868): 297–306. For Oakland, consult Jack J. Studer, "Julius Kellersberger: A Swiss as Surveyor and City Planner in California, 1851–1857," *California Historical Society Quarterly* 47 (March 1968): 3–14, and Jack S. Studer, "The First Map of Oakland, California: An Historical Speculation as Solution to an Enigma," *California Historical Society Quarterly* 48 (March 1969): 59–71. The beginnings of Modesto and Fresno are described in Solomon P. Elias, *Stories of Stanislaus* (Modesto, Calif., 1924), and Paul E. Vandor, *History of Fresno County, California* (Los Angeles, 1919).

86. *The West Shore* (September 1883): 204. See Quiett, *They Built the West*, pp. 339–99, for helpful material on the impact of railroads in Portland.

others. This period also saw the planning of the university towns of Berkeley and Palo Alto, the further growth of Oakland and Sacramento, and the creation by railroad land companies of such cities along the Southern Pacific line through the San Joaquin Valley as Fresno (Figure 82) and Modesto.[85]

The introduction of rail transportation brought a renewed burst of urban expansion and city planning in the Pacific Northwest as well. Portland residents had long and impatiently awaited a direct link with the East to replace inadequate connections by ship to San Francisco or by combinations of railroad and stagecoach routes south through the Willamette valley or east along the Columbia River. After the first train of the Northern Pacific arrived in 1883, a local editor could justifiably claim that "in the extent and convenience of her railroad facilities Portland has no rival in the northwest."[86] The Union Pacific reached the city the following year, and both lines contributed substantially to Portland's industrial and commercial expansion during the balance of the decade (Figure 83).

The railroad era of the Northwest region included the usual town-founding activities of the major lines. Such places as Cheney (Figure 84) and Yakima, planned by railroad land subsidiaries in the 1880s, added to the growing number of communities that had by that time given Washington and Oregon an extensive network of urban settlement. Almost all of these communities had been established by speculators who, following the custom of the American frontier, surveyed their sites in grid designs of routine character.

Only the original and discarded plan for Tacoma deviated from this approach. There, in 1873, the Northern Pacific engaged Frederick Law Olmsted to prepare a plan for a new city that would serve as the Pacific terminus of the line. Olmsted's plan with its curving streets leading across the contours to provide easy gradients to and from the waterfront reflected the steep slopes of the site (Figure 85). It also, of course, represented Olmsted's fascination with the romantic plan forms that derived from English garden design and that he had used with such skill in the planning of New York's Central Park and of the suburban community of Riverside, Illinois, perhaps his finest essay in town planning.

For a railroad terminus, however, his Tacoma design was a curiously inept proposal. A single railroad line leading up a small wharf is the only hint

Figure 83. Portland, Oregon, in 1890

Published & Copyrighted 1884 by J.J.STONER, Madison Wis.

SOUTH SIDE OF FIRST STREET, FROM A TO G STREETS.

BIRD'S EYE VIEW OF

CHENEY, WASH. TER.

COUNTY SEAT OF SPOKANE COUNTY.

1884

BECK & PAULI, LITHO. Milwaukee Wis.

CHENEY COLLEGE

1—Cheney College.
2—County Court House.
3—Congregational Church.
4—Baptist Church.
5—Catholic Church.
6—Methodist Church.
7—Flouring Mill.
8—Oakes House, McMurtagh, Prop.
9—Commercial Hotel, John Norris, Prop.
10—Sp——ane Co. Bank, Danford & Co, D. Ainsworth Cash.
12—Bavaria Brewery, Weber & Forster.
13—N. P. R. R. Passenger Depot.
14—N. P. R. R. Freight Depot.
15—Livery, Feed and Sale Stable, F. F. Clark, Prop.
16—Opera House, W. W. Griswold, Prop.
17—Range & Addlton.

D. F. Percival, Real Estate and General Business Agent, cor. Second and R. st.
J. F. Parks, Attorney at Law, F. st.
T. M. Calloway, Real Estate, First st.
J. H. Hughes & Co., Hardware, Stoves and Agricultural Implements, First st., cor. F
J. H. Range, Real Estate Agent, and Justice of the Peace, First st.
H. W. Pruner, Blacksmith and Wagon shop, First st., cor. F.
N. Knutneky & Son, General Merchandise, First st., cor. F
W. W. Griswold, Billiard Parlor, First st.
F. A. Pomeroy, Physician and Surgeon, First st.

W. G. Barney, Attorney at Law, First st
W. B. Switzer, Drugs, Books, Stationery, etc., First st.
Peter Bettinger, General Merchandise, First st., cor. D
J. W. Johnson, Physician and Surgeon, First st.
J. H. Walter, Manufacturer of Saddles, Harness, etc., First st
D. E. French, Dealer in Lumber, etc., Railroad st.
M. B. Whitney, Physician and Surgeon, First st.
H. B. Mason, Saloon and Billiard Hall, First st.
Geo. W. Eastman, Barber and Bath Rooms, First st.
Wm. Straub, New York Bakery and Restaurant, First st.
Joseph Brooks, Confectionery, Cigars, Tobacco, etc., R. st. cor. M. R. st

P. F. Underholm, Furniture and Undertaking, F—— st.
R. C. Gregg, Drug, st. First st.
J. Cassert, Groceries, Crockery, etc., First st.
Mrs. J. B. Swanson, Restaurant, First st.
G. W. Settlemier, Groceries and Provisions, First st
J. B. Bosey, Manufacturer of Wagons, Carriages, Sleighs etc., Second ——, cor. F
A. Bielgen, Furniture and Undertaking, First st., cor. B
J. Ritter, Contractor and Builder, First st., cor. A
E. Wilson, Lumber Yard, First st., cor. Overlain.
Louis Maine, Dealer in Harvesting Machinery, R st.
F. J. Harms, Photographer, First st.
S. F. Sohan, Editor Northwest Tribune, D St., cor Second
J. F. Spencer, Editor Cheney Sentinel, First st.
Percival & Andros, Railroad Land and Real Estate Agents, office in N. P. R. R. Passenger Depot.

Figure 84. Cheney, Washington, in 1884

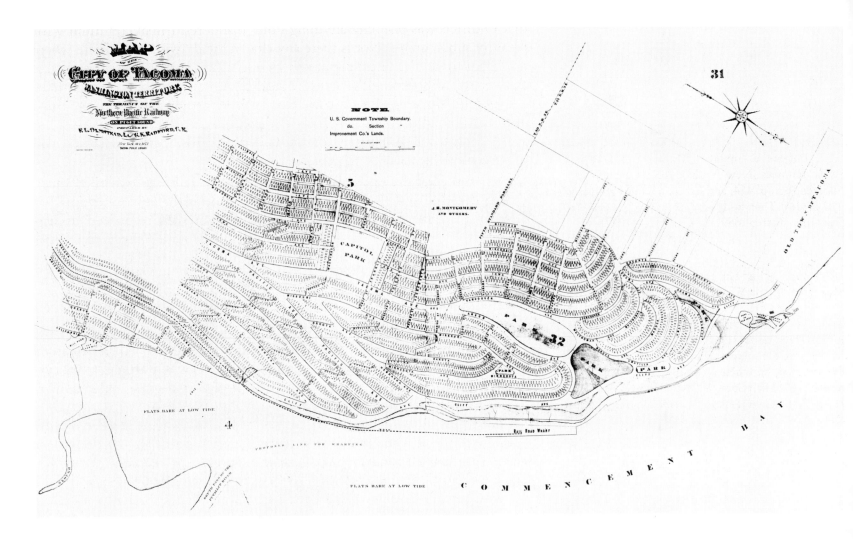

Figure 85. Frederick Law Olmsted's plan for Tacoma, Washington, in 1873

that Olmsted was planning anything other than a residential community for wealthy suburbanites. Nor is there any clue in the drawing to indicate where the business district or public buildings might be located. Several parks are shown, but no sites for schools are indicated. Although Olmsted might have successfully modified his basic concept with further study, the company turned instead to one of its engineers for a gridiron plan of surpassing dullness but with ample accommodations for rail lines and yards, docks, wharves, and other facilities needed for a major port.[87]

Only a few of the new towns built by Western railroads exhibited much skill in urban design or care in development. Almost the only exception was Colorado Springs, founded by Gen. William J. Palmer as a resort and residential showplace on his narrow-gauge Denver and Rio Grande line. Here Palmer fulfilled the usual claims of the townsite speculator by actually constructing a luxury hotel, opera house, churches, and college, planting hundreds of trees, and constructing a modern water supply system.

While Palmer used a basic grid pattern, he laid it out in more than routine fashion (Figure 86). He saw to it that the 140-foot-wide Pike's Peak Avenue terminated at the hotel site, with the towering mountain for which he named the street providing a dramatic vista in the distance. Twin diagonal streets cutting across the grid also focused on the hotel, although they ended a short distance away at block-square parks.

Under Palmer's watchful guidance Colorado Springs proved to be a profitable venture, demonstrating that sound planning and generous development policies were not necessarily incompatible with economic success (Figure 87). It was only here, however, that Palmer pursued this enlightened program, for elsewhere on his line he created a series of dreary little grid settlements of no merit whatsoever.[88]

CITIES OF ZION

While in large portions of the American West the railroads thrust their tracks through unsettled regions, the central section of the Union Pacific line passed across the northern edge of an area that was already occupied and where by

87. Eugene V. Smalley, *History of the Northern Pacific Railroad* (New York, 1883); Quiett, *They Built the West*, p. 414; and Tacoma Land Company, *The Western Terminus of the Northern Pacific Railroad* (Tacoma, Wash., 1889).

88. A brief but enlightening review of Palmer's career is Brit Allan Storey, "William Jackson Palmer, Promoter," *Colorado Magazine* 42 (Winter 1966): 44–55. Palmer's role in founding and developing Colorado Springs and the later history of that city are the subject of a fine book I unaccountably overlooked when writing *Cities of the American West*: Marshall Sprague, *Newport in the Rockies: The Life and Good Times of Colorado Springs* (Denver, 1961). Other towns planned by Palmer's railroad included South Pueblo, Durango, and Salida. Early views of the first two are reproduced in Reps, *Cities of the American West*, figs. 17.18, 17.19, and 17.20, pp. 584–86. See also pp. 583 and 589–91 for a more complete treatment of the planning of Colorado Springs.

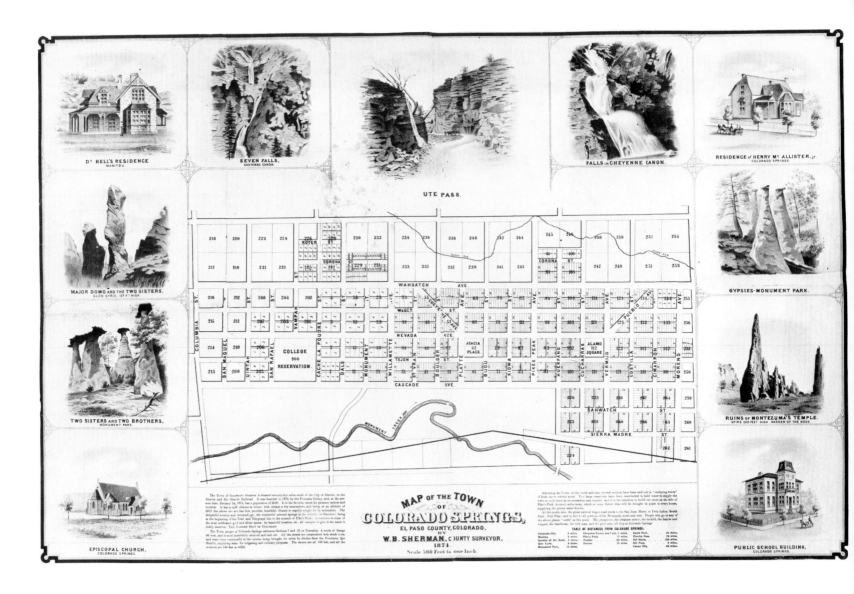

Figure 86. Colorado Springs, Colorado, in 1874, as planned by William J. Palmer

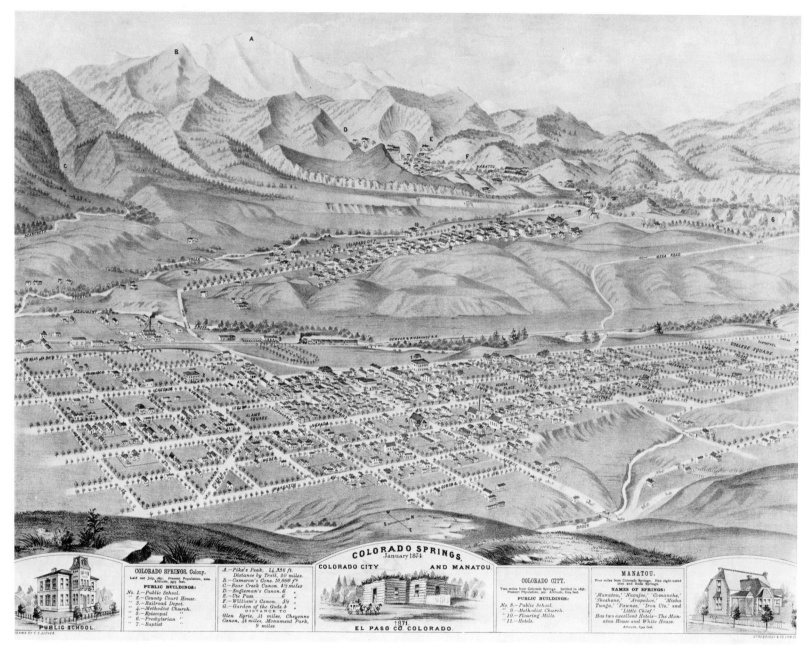

Figure 87. Colorado Springs, Colorado, in 1874

1869 well over one hundred planned towns provided the focus of an agricultural and industrial economy. This was the Great Basin domain of the Mormons, whose settlement of Utah and the surrounding lands began in 1847 under the leadership of Brigham Young.

The mass exodus to Utah started in Nauvoo, Illinois, in a final effort by the Mormons to escape religious discrimination and persecution. Their plight was not new. From their earliest center in Fayette, New York, where Joseph Smith had founded the new religious sect, they had been forced to move to Kirtland, Ohio, and then to Missouri. There, at Far West and Adam-ondi-Ahman, Mormon leaders surveyed new towns according to a design that Smith first devised in 1833 for the intended City of Zion near Independence, a small community not far from Kansas City.[89]

Smith's plan called for a mile-square grid of streets, each 132 feet wide, with three large squares at the center of the grid (Figure 88). One of these squares was to be used for the bishop's storehouses, and twelve temples were to be constructed on each of the other two. Farm fields were to be located beyond the town's boundaries, but all members of the settlement were to live in the town. Its most unusual and inexplicable feature was the system of dividing the blocks into building sites so that the resulting lots faced in alternating directions as one passed along a street from block to block.

Driven from Missouri by new outbreaks of violence, the Mormons fled to a location on the Illinois bank of the Mississippi where Smith planned Nauvoo in 1839, although here he did not use the City of Zion design as a guide (Figure 89). Nauvoo soon became the largest city in Illinois as thousands of new converts joined the community or settled in the smaller Mormon-planned town of Ramus in Illinois or in two villages on the Iowa side of the river. Confident of his position and security in this rapidly growing and impressive city with its huge temple, Smith in 1842 revealed his doctrine of plural marriage. This created new hostilities within and without the church and led to Smith's death at the hands of a mob in 1844. Further outrages followed, and Brigham Young, the new leader of the church, determined to abandon Nauvoo and move all of his fellow Mormons to Utah.

This painful hegira began early in 1846 when Young led the vanguard of his flock across the frozen Mississippi to Iowa and set out to establish the temporary community of Winter Quarters, Nebraska, on the western bank of the

89. The literature of Mormon history is vast. A few of the better-known works are cited in the Bibliographical Note. Many others are noted in the two chapters of Reps, *Cities of the American West*, that treat Mormon town planning in far more detail than is possible here. See pp. 313–42 and the forty-two plans, maps, and views of Mormon towns that appear with the text. Two bibliographies should be consulted by the reader seeking a guide to Mormon history: Philip A. M. Tayler, "Recent Writing on Utah and the Mormons," *Arizona and the West* 4 (Autumn 1962): 249–60; and Thomas G. Alexander and James B. Allen, "The Mormons in the Mountain West: A Selected Bibliography," *Arizona and the West* 9 (Winter 1967): 365–84.

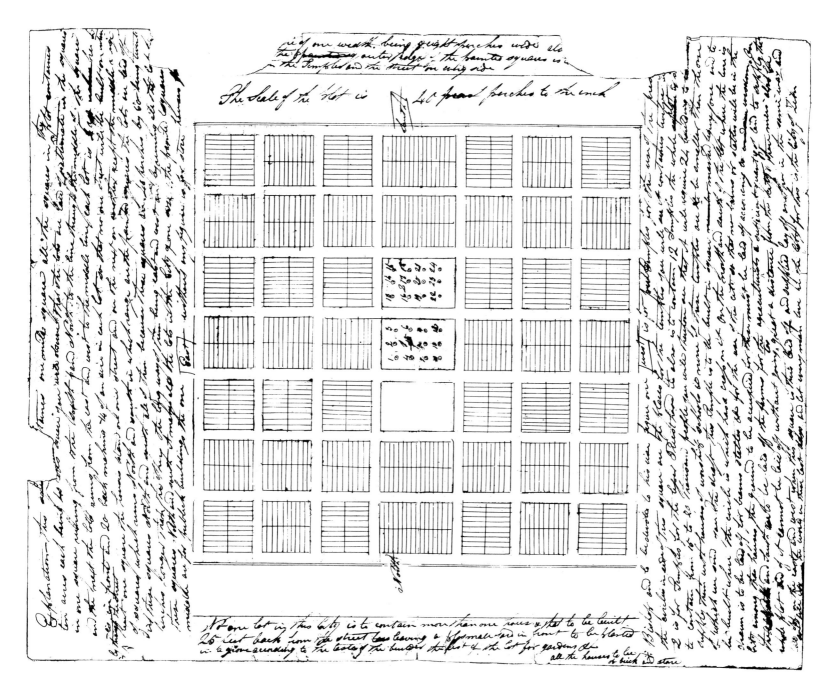

Figure 88. Joseph Smith's plan in 1833 for the Mormon City of Zion near Independence, Missouri

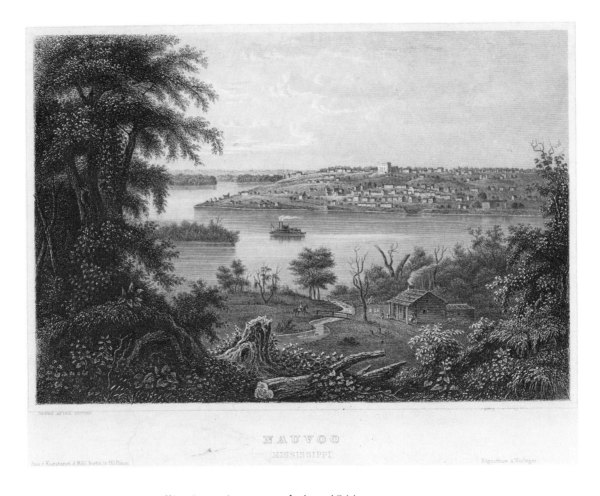

NAUVOO
MISSISSIPPI

Figure 89. Nauvoo, Illinois, as it appeared circa 1844

Missouri. With a picked group of followers, Young pushed on the next spring to the barren shores of Great Salt Lake. There, late in July 1847, he marked off the streets, blocks, temple site, public squares, and building lots of Salt Lake City in a pattern similar to Smith's City of Zion (Figure 90). By mid-October the new city's population exceeded two thousand, and the residents were busy constructing cabins and breaking ground for crops to be planted in the rectangular farm fields surveyed under Young's direction beyond the urban nucleus.

Salt Lake City provided a model for most of the other Mormon communities planned during the ensuing years elsewhere in Utah as well as in Nevada, Arizona, Wyoming, Montana, and as far distant as San Bernardino, California (Figure 91). It was a remarkable and unprecedented achievement in the history of planning. By the end of their first decade in the Great Basin region the Mormons had surveyed and occupied more than one hundred new towns. When Brigham Young died in 1877, 358 had been established, and at the end of the century at least 500 of these communities had been created.

Such accomplishments were not fortuitous, for Young and his associates adopted a policy of town development that left little to chance. First a general location for a new settlement was selected that could accommodate additional population growth. Then an exploring party was dispatched to select the most favorable specific site. From Salt Lake City and other established communities, members of the church with the needed skills were "called" by Young to lead the first cohort of settlers. They received the necessary tools and implements from the church storehouse, along with seeds and enough food to suffice for the first few months.

At the site, such as Provo (Figure 92), the cadre constructed a fortified enclosure to provide temporary accommodations over the first winter and staked out the agricultural allotments nearby. In the spring the surveyor laid out the streets and blocks, and town lots and farm fields were distributed to the residents. In many cases Brigham Young presided at this event, coming from Salt Lake City with other church officials for the occasion.

Virtually all of these early Mormon towns still exist, testifying to the skills used in their site selection, the care taken in their planning, the systematic manner in which they were supplied and encouraged, and the determination of their settlers to build communities even under unfavorable circumstances

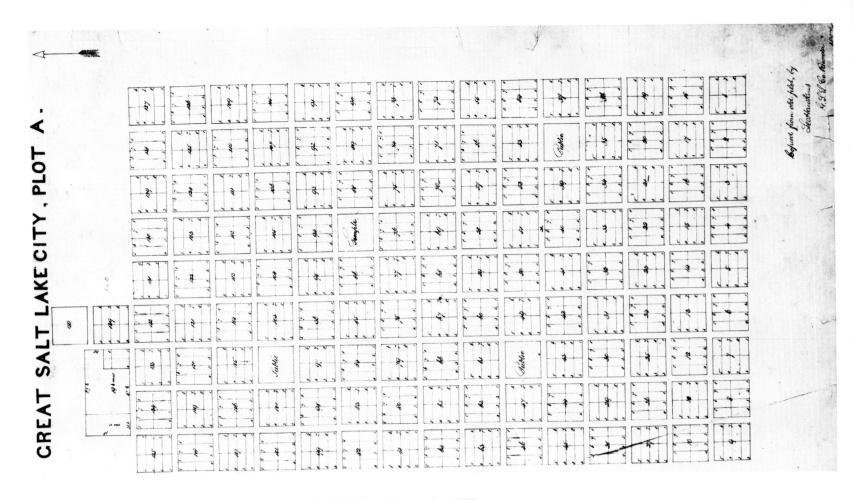

Figure 90. Salt Lake City, Utah, as planned by Brigham Young in 1847

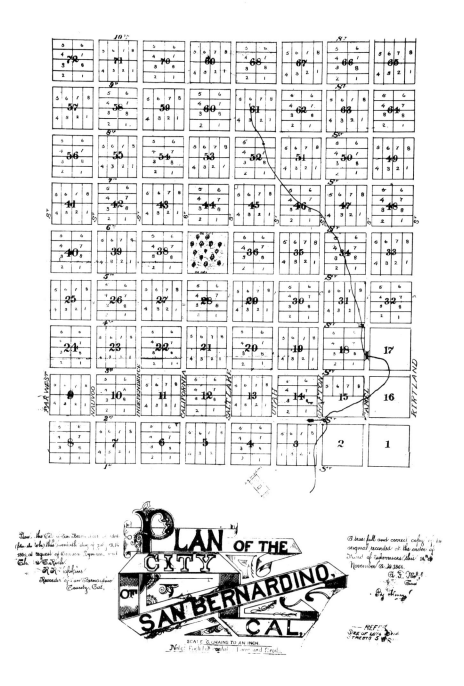

Figure 91. San Bernardino, California, in 1854

FORT UTAH ON THE TIMPANOGAS.   VALLEY OF THE GREAT SALT LAKE.

Figure 92. Fort Utah at Provo, Utah, in 1849

and with limited resources. Many of these towns are, of course, of modest size, such as Manti (Figure 93) and St. George, although the latter is one of the four temple cities of Utah.

Others, like Mesa, Arizona, surveyed in 1878, did not enjoy substantial growth until well into the twentieth century (Figure 94). It, too, is now a temple city, an imposing structure for that purpose having been completed in 1927. Although many towns were planned by the Mormons elsewhere in Arizona, the main concentration of Mormon urbanization occupies a series of valleys that extends northward from Provo to Logan, a distance of about one hundred miles. Dominating this once near-desert region is Salt Lake City, the spiritual, political, and economic heart of the Great Basin. Slightly more than a century ago, when Young last saw it, it had become a city of sixteen thousand and had expanded even beyond the generous boundaries he had provided (Figure 95).

Urban planning was thus an essential element in opening lands for agriculture in the Mormon domain. Mormon towns, at least in the initial decades, not only furnished places for trade, recreation, worship, and education—as did other communities in the West—but they also provided farmers, in addition to those working in other occupations, with their place of residence. The Mormon settlement, like settlements in early New England and in the Hispanic West, united town and country in regions where urban and rural occupation occurred simultaneously.

TOWNS IN A RUSH

The final spurt of Western town founding before 1890 took place under conditions sharply contrasting with the orderly and well-organized procedure adopted by the Mormons. It also opened for settlement the last area of the region available for development. Whatever lessons had been learned about town planning in the American West were forgotten in the thoughtless manner by which white settlers were allowed to occupy a strategic portion of the Indian lands in Oklahoma in 1889.

Pressure to allow settlement in Oklahoma had built up steadily with the growth of population in Texas, Arkansas, Kansas, and Missouri. To this area

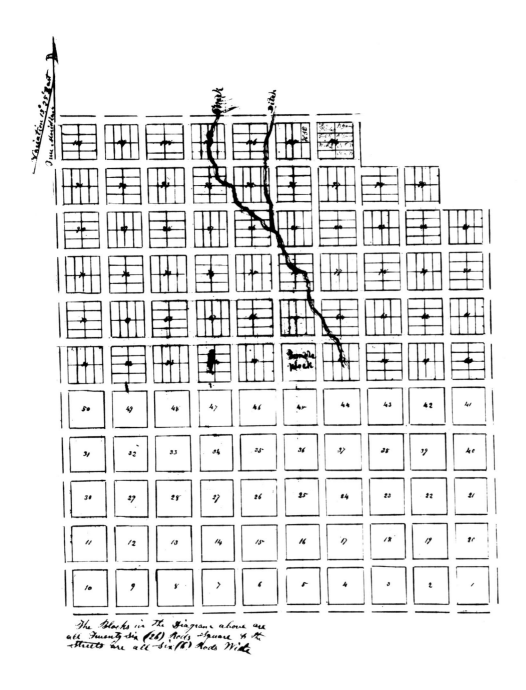

Figure 93. Manti, Utah, in 1850

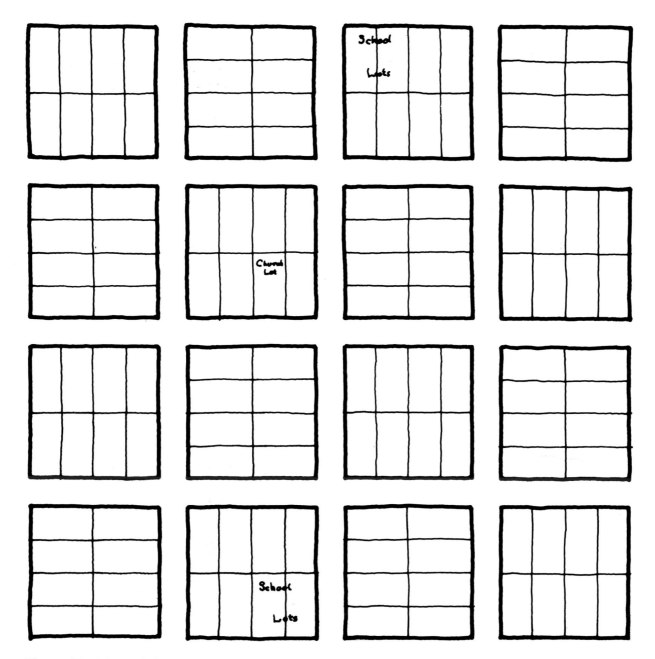

Figure 94. Mesa, Arizona, as planned in 1878

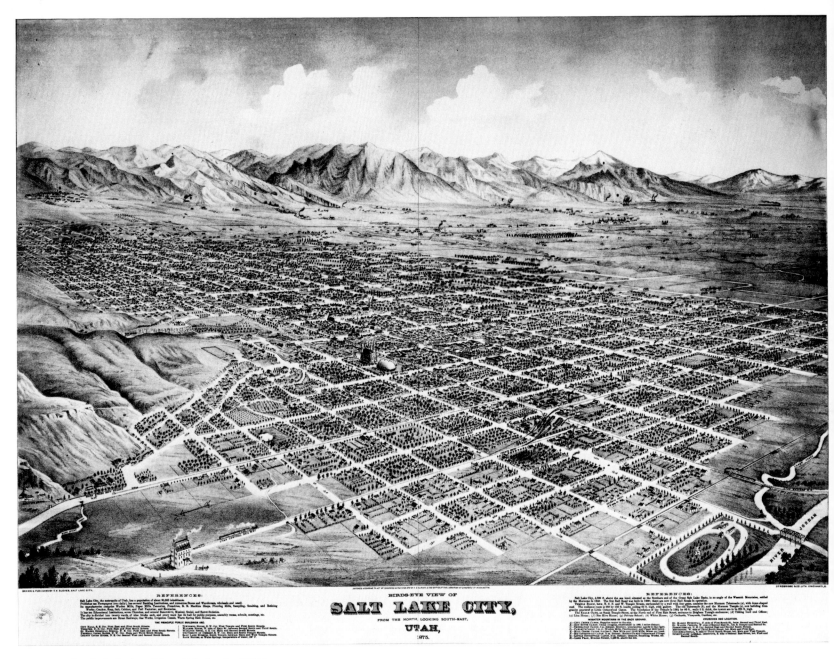

DRAWN & PUBLISHED BY E.S. GLOVER, SALT LAKE CITY.

REFERENCES:

Salt Lake City, the metropolis of Utah, has a population of about 20,000 inhabitants.

Publishes ten Newspapers (two daily), has several Banking Institutions, and numerous Stores and Warehouses, wholesale and retail.

Its manufactures comprise Woolen Mills, Paper Mills, Tanneries, Foundries, R. R. Machine Shops, Flouring Mills, Sampling, Smelting, and Refining Works; Cracker, Soap, Salt, Candles, and Pail Factories; and Breweries.

It has ten Educational Institutions, seven Churches, and several Benevolent, Musical, Social, and Sacret Societies.

The city is divided into twenty wards, of nine blocks each, and every ward has its hall for public purposes, assembly rooms, schools, meetings, etc.

The public improvements are Street Railways, Gas Works, Irrigation Canals, Warm Spring Bath House, etc.

THE PRINCIPLE PUBLIC BUILDINGS ARE.

City Hall, S. E. Cor. First East and First South Streets.

Theatre, E. E. Cor. First East and First South Streets.

U. S. Marshall Superintendent's Office, N. E. Cor. First East and First South Streets.

Federal Court House, S. W. Cor. Main and Third South Streets.

Deseret Court House, S. E. Cor. Second West and Second South Streets.

University, E. W. Cor. Main and North Temple Streets.

Salt Lake Museum, South Temple, between Main and West Temple Streets.

Bath House, at Warm Springs, temperature of water, 128° F.

ENTERED ACCORDING TO ACT OF CONGRESS IN THE YEAR 1875 BY E. S. GLOVER, IN THE OFFICE OF THE LIBRARIAN OF CONGRESS AT WASHINGTON.

BIRDS-EYE VIEW OF
SALT LAKE CITY,
UTAH,
FROM THE NORTH, LOOKING SOUTH-EAST,
1875.

STROBRIDGE & CO. LITH. CINCINNATI, O.

REFERENCES:

Salt Lake City, 4,300 ft. above the sea level, situated at the Southern end of the Great Salt Lake Basin, in an angle of the Wasatch Mountains, settled by the Mormons in 1847. The first Rail Road was built in 1869; there are now three Rail Roads in operation.

Temple Block, here, N. S. E. and W. Temple Streets, surrounded by a wall four gates, contains the new Mormon Tabernacle (a), with dome shaped roof. The audience room is 250 by 150 ft. inside, ceiling 65 ft. high, with gallery. The old Tabernacle (b), and the Mormon Temple (c), now building from granite quarried at Little Cottonwood Canon. The foundation of the Temple is 16 ft. wide, walls 8 ft. thick, the towers are to be 220 ft. high.

The Endowment House (d), Tithing Yard and Offices; the Endowment House, on South Temple Street, at the North end of First East Street.

(e) Elias House; (f) Bee Hive House; (g) Private School; (h) White House; (i) Orchards, Vineyards, Gardens, etc.

WASATCH MOUNTAINS ON THE BACK GROUND.

(1) City Creek Canon, Supplies water to the city.

(2) Ensign Peak, Camp Douglas, established in 1862, 3 miles distant.

(3) Emigration Canon, 4 m. distant. Emigrants Guide to the right.

(4) Great Mill Creek, 1 m. J. Woolen Mills, Distillery and Paper Mill here.

(5) Big Cotton Wood Canon, 6 m.; Saw Mills and North Temple Streets.

(6) Little Cottonwood Canon, 12 m. distant, Reservoir and Cottonwood Village.

(7) Jordan Overflow. Canal, 12 m. distant, Granite Smelting Works, etc.

(8) Lone Peak, Wasatch Range, 11,326 ft. above the sea.

CHURCHES AND LOCATION.

St. Marks Episcopal, S. side of South Temple St., near Second and Third East.

St. Pauls, Catholic, W. side of Second East St., bet. S. Temple and Second St.

Presbyterian, N. E. Cor. Second East and Second South Streets.

Methodist, W. side of Third South Street, bet. Main and First East.

Congregational, S. side of Third South Street, bet. Main and First East.

New Jerusalem, N. side of Second East Street, bet. First and Second South.

Figure 95. Salt Lake City, Utah, in 1875

134 · The Forgotten Frontier

the United States government had moved many Indian tribes from elsewhere in the West to join such Southeastern Indians as the Cherokees, Creeks, Choctaws, Chickasaws, and Seminoles who had been forcibly relocated there from 1817 to 1842. Supposedly permanent treaties guaranteed perpetual title to these tribes and prohibited settlers from encroaching on their lands.

A major part of the Indian Territory in central Oklahoma, nearly 2 million acres in size, had not been designated for any individual tribe and was known as the Unassigned Lands. It was to this location that the advocates of white settlement, led by the fanatical and tireless David L. Payne, directed their attention. As early as 1880 Payne mounted his first invasion of the area, leading a group of "Boomers" to a location in what is now Oklahoma City and quickly surveying a townsite before being removed by federal troops. At least eight other attempts by Payne ended in similar fashion, and it was his death in 1884, rather than any lessened eagerness to settle in Oklahoma on the part of his followers, that led to a temporary halt in these illegal incursions.[90]

Shifting their attention to Washington, proponents of Oklahoma settlement pressured the Congress and the president for legislation to allow occupation of the Unassigned Lands in accordance with the existing homestead and townsite provisions of the laws governing the disposition of the public domain. Their efforts were rewarded in 1889 when Congress passed a law allowing the president to open the lands by proclamation, and Pres. Benjamin Harrison designated noon on 22 April as the earliest moment for legal entry to the lands.

Congress neglected to provide for any system of civil government in this area, although federal land offices were established at some of the depots of the Santa Fé Railroad, which had been completed between Kansas and Texas two years earlier. Nor had any townsites been surveyed, even though it was clear that the most desirable places for new communities would be at and around the depots. And while the law specified that only federal marshals and railroad employees were to be allowed within the limits of the Unassigned Lands before the appointed time, hundreds, perhaps thousands, of so-called Sooners invaded the area and concealed themselves near desirable locations for towns and homesteads. As it turned out, they found themselves in stiff competition with railroad employees, officials of the federal government, and others who brazenly and often successfully claimed land despite a provision that they were ineligible to do so.[91]

90. Payne's activities are set against this background in Carl Coke Rister, *Land Hunger: David L. Payne and the Oklahoma Boomers* (Norman, Okla., 1942).

91. B. B. Chapman, "The Legal Sooners of 1889 in Oklahoma," *Chronicles of Oklahoma* 35 (Winter 1957–1958): 328–415. Chapman is the author of many other valuable articles on this episode in Oklahoma's history, all of them appearing in the *Chronicles of Oklahoma*: "Guthrie, from Public Land to Private Property," 33 (Spring 1955): 63–86; "Oklahoma City, from Public Land to Private Property," 37 (Summer 1959): 211–37, (Autumn 1959): 33–52, (Winter 1959–1960): 440–79; "Opening the Cherokee Outlet: An Archival Study," 40 (Summer 1962): 158–81, (Autumn 1962): 253–85; "Perkins Townsite: An Archival Case Study," 25 (Summer 1947): 82–91; "The Enid 'Railroad War': An Archival Study," 43 (Summer 1965): 126–94; and "The Founding of El Reno," 34 (Spring 1956): 79–108. See also his *The Founding of Stillwater* (Oklahoma City, 1948).

At noon on the appointed day, signal shots set off a mad rush by tens of thousands of persons impatiently gathered at the Kansas and Texas borders. They came on foot, by horse, and on trains so crowded that the car roofs were occupied and many were left behind at the starting points. At their destinations they hit the ground in full stride to begin a confusing search for unclaimed land (Figure 96). By the time most of them reached Guthrie, as one correspondent reported, "the slope east of the railway . . . was dotted white with tents and sprinkled thick with men running about in all directions."[92]

Townsite companies whose officers were illegal Sooners had already platted two 320-acre sites at Guthrie Station. Members of other townsite groups arriving by train extended these street lines into the prairies for a distance of some two miles from the depot (Figure 97). By nightfall enough town lots had been staked off for a city of perhaps one hundred thousand residents, although the number of persons then present probably did not exceed one-tenth of that number.[93]

At Oklahoma Station another band of Sooners slipped past the border guards and completed staking out an entire half square mile as Oklahoma City within less than an hour after the official opening of the territory. By midafternoon their representative appeared at the Guthrie land office to file a townsite application. The first legal entrants to reach the area were forced to survey their plat to the south of this earlier claim. The following day it became apparent that the two townsites overlapped, and after a mass meeting of the conflicting parties an elected committee began the almost impossible task of reconciling the two surveys. A series of unsightly and inconvenient jogs or street offsets, recorded in the first printed map of Oklahoma City (Figure 98), as well as in the earliest view of the city (Figure 99), can still be found in the city's business district where the two plats met, conflicted, and were finally adjusted.[94]

Elsewhere on the eventful day towns were planned under similar conditions at Norman (Figure 100), El Reno, and Kingfisher. A month later on an eighty-acre tract that had somehow been overlooked, a town was planned at Stillwater, which was enlarged to 240 acres when claimants of adjoining homesteads agreed to include their land. All of these towns, like Guthrie and Oklahoma City, were thus designed under such hectic circumstances as to

92. The quotation is from a vivid, accurate, and fascinating eyewitness account in a respected and reliable Eastern journal. See William Willard Howard, "The Rush to Oklahoma," *Harper's Weekly* 33 (18 May 1889): 391–94. It includes several revealing views of Guthrie's appearance on its first day of existence. For another journalist's report of the period, see Hamilton S. Wicks, "The Opening of Oklahoma," *The Cosmopolitan* 7 (September 1889): 460–70.

93. Howard, "The Rush to Oklahoma," p. 391. One of the two first townsites was East Guthrie, founded by a Winfield, Kansas, group who brought to Oklahoma a "survey" made from a train window ten days earlier by their surveyor who also relied on his memories from visits to the area a year before. Two hundred members of this group concealed themselves near the station and precisely at noon emerged to occupy the site and stake it off. See testimony in the case of *Townsite Settlers of East Guthrie* v. *Veeder B. Paine et al.*, as quoted in Chapman, "Guthrie," p. 71. For Guthrie's founding and early years, see Gerald Forbes, *Guthrie: Oklahoma's First Capital* (Norman, Okla., 1938).

94. For the chaotic situation at Oklahoma City and its ultimate resolution, see A. W. Durham, "Oklahoma City before the Run of 1889," *Chronicles of Oklahoma* 36 (Spring 1958): 72–78; Angelo C. Scott, *The Story of Oklahoma City* (Oklahoma City, 1939); and Chapman, "Oklahoma City."

LAYING OUT TOWN LOTS IN GUTHRIE, TWENTY MINUTES AFTER THE ARRIVAL OF THE FIRST TRAIN.

Figure 96. Guthrie, Oklahoma, on the opening day of the land rush in 1889

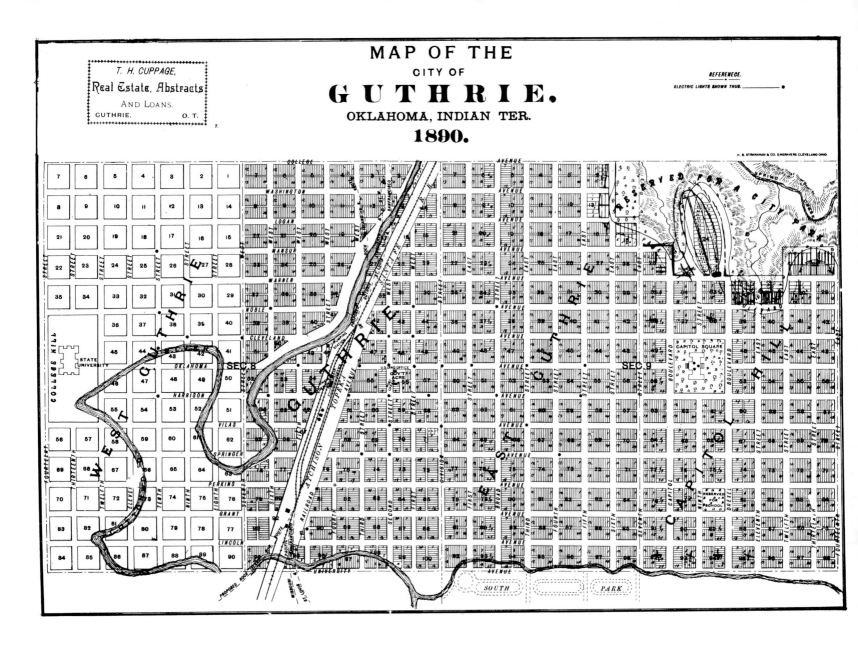

Figure 97. The four townsites planned at Guthrie, Oklahoma, in 1889

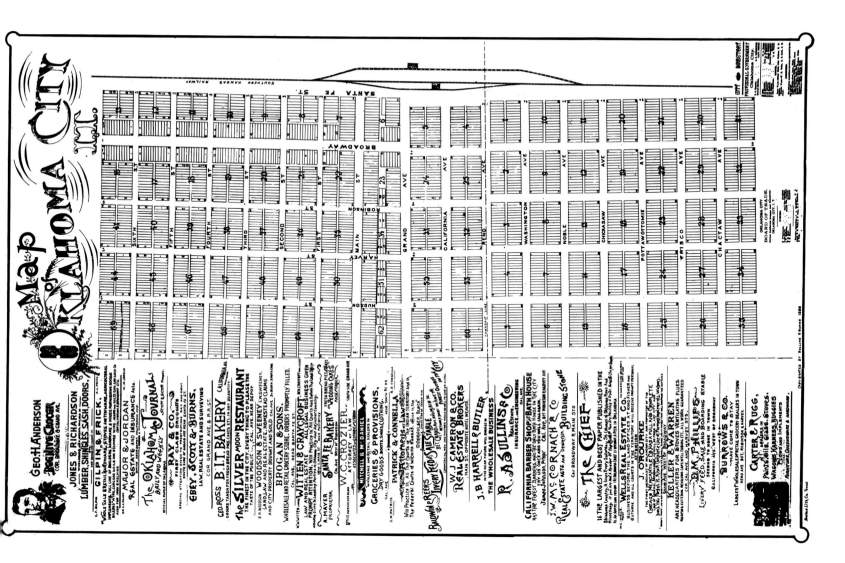

Figure 98. Oklahoma City, Oklahoma, as planned in 1889

Figure 99. Oklahoma City, Oklahoma, in 1890, ten months after the land rush

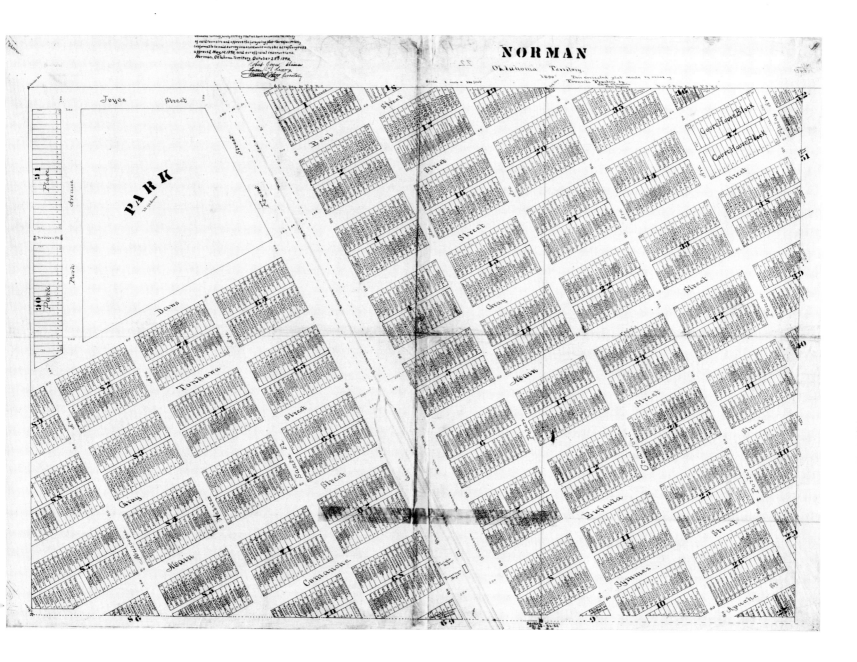

Figure 100. Norman, Oklahoma, as planned in 1899

preclude any but the most mechanical, monotonous, and routine designs. And the results were almost identical in the subsequent land rushes and auctions used to dispose of other Oklahoma lands reluctantly surrendered by Indian tribes.[95]

URBAN GROWTH AND
THE TEMPER OF THE WEST

A year before the institutionalized chaos of the first Oklahoma land rush a perceptive English observer and a warm friend of America published a remarkable study of the United States. In his *American Commonwealth*, James Bryce devoted a chapter to what he termed "The Temper of the West." While he stated his admiration for the energy and skills displayed by Western pioneers, he also felt troubled by the mania for speculation, the wasteful exploitation of resources, and the "passionate eagerness . . . towards the material development of the country" that was so absorbing "that it almost ceases to be selfish . . . [and] . . . takes from its very vastness a tinge of ideality."[96]

Bryce found it strange and self-deluding that every village or small city yearned to become a great metropolis. When he attended the cornerstone ceremonies for the capitol at Bismarck, North Dakota, he was struck by the fact that the building was located nearly a mile away from the town on a rise in the prairie (Figure 58). When he asked if the intention was to surround the structure with a great park, he was told, "'By no means; the Capitol is intended to be in the centre of the city; it is in this direction that the city is to grow.'"

Noting that this attitude was "the same everywhere from the Mississippi to the Pacific," Bryce addressed a series of searching questions to his American friends: "Why sacrifice the present to the future, fancying that you will be happier when your fields teem with wealth and your cities with people? In Europe we have cities wealthier and more populous than yours, and we are not happy. . . . Why, then, seek to complete in a few decades what the older nations of the world took thousands of years over in the older continents? Why do things rudely and ill which need to be done well, seeing that the welfare of your descendants may turn upon them?"

95. A useful general study of the origins of these first towns in Oklahoma is John Alley, *City Beginnings in Oklahoma Territory* (Norman, Okla., 1939). Later land rushes were those of 1891, when the townsites of Chandler and Tecumseh were surveyed in advance; 1892; 1893, with the townsites of Pond Creek, Enid, Perry, Newkirk, and Alva also being planned by government surveyors beforehand; and 1895. In 1901 on former Indian lands in southwestern Oklahoma federal surveyors laid out Anadarko, Lawton, and Hobart, and lots were auctioned.

96. James Bryce, *The American Commonwealth*, 3d ed. (New York, 1907), 2: 833. In the revisions since its first publication in London in 1888, the chapter on the West remained unaltered.

Somberly, Bryce concluded his observations on the American West:

> Politically, and perhaps socially also, this haste and excitement, this absorption in the development of the material resources of the country, are unfortunate. As a town built in a hurry is seldom well built, so a society will be the sounder in health for not having grown too swiftly. Doubtless much of the scum will be cleared away from the surface when the liquid settles and cools down. . . . Nevertheless . . . the unrestfulness, the passion for speculation, the feverish eagerness for quick and showy results, may so soak into the texture of the popular mind as to colour it for centuries to come. These are the shadows which to the eye of the traveller seem to fall across the glowing landscape of the Great West.[97]

97. Ibid., pp. 637–39.

Although the two men addressed themselves to somewhat different issues, subsequent events and further historical research show that it was Bryce and not Turner who was the more perceptive interpreter of the meaning of the Western experience. Bryce's observations about the motivating forces in Western expansion and their probable consequences nowhere have greater validity than when applied to city development. Turner's hypothesis, on the other hand, offers almost nothing to the student of Western urbanization.

How might the Turner hypothesis be reformulated to accommodate this evidence of towns as the vanguard of settlement and the ubiquity of urban planning as the method for their creation? How, in short, should the historian of city planning interpret the effect of the frontier on the American character? Such an interpretation might begin with an assertion that the fresh opportunities afforded by the frontier lay as much in townsite promotion and urban-based enterprise as in farming. It would certainly recognize that the vaunted democratic traits of Turner's frontiersman were shaped not so much by noninstitutionalized cooperative efforts connected with creating rural societies as by the more demanding and intricate tasks of erecting municipal governments and guiding the affairs of new states and territories.

Surely, too, much of the self-reliance that Turner saw as deriving from the experience of lonely farmers carving the prairies into fields for crops must have come also from the efforts of town-dwellers who were learning to plan cities, managing the problems of urban health and sanitation, building the structures and institutions needed to accommodate urban growth, providing schools and churches, arranging for fire and police protection, and lobbying in territorial and state legislatures to have their town designated as a county seat or a capital or as the location of an infant university.

Perhaps we are left only with Turner's doctrine that as the frontier moved westward European influences on society weakened, and at the end the men and women of the frontier emerged as thoroughly Americanized—unsophisticated, direct, guileless. In the plans for Western towns there is much to suggest that the more elaborate and varied designs for such colonial settlements as Philadelphia, New Haven, Williamsburg, Annapolis, and Savannah, as well as the baroque plan for Washington and its partial derivatives at Buffalo, Detroit, Indianapolis, and Madison, were ignored as models by frontier planners. Instead, most Western towns were planned in patterns that progressively moved toward standardization based on the undeviating grid. From Santa Fe to Oklahoma City there are, sadly, fewer exceptions to this generalization than one might wish.

Much of what concerned Bryce about frontier values and attitudes remains, as he suggested it might, still deeply ingrained in the American mind. This is reflected in an unwillingness to recognize that resources are finite and rapidly becoming scarce, in a belief that bigness is necessarily better, and in a failure to understand that no longer can one flee to some new location leaving behind unsolved or mismanaged problems of the environment. The massive suburbanization of recent decades is only the latest manifestation of a long-outmoded frontier mentality.

All the energy and determination that Western pioneers applied to town founding and development—and far greater skills and imagination—will be required to solve the perplexing problems facing America's cities today, not only in those instant communities of the West but also throughout the country. History extends a heavy hand, and we still are held within its grasp. To loosen its tightened fingers Americans will need creative but realistic visions of an urban future as inspiring as those dreams of power, wealth, freedom, conquest, and opportunity that led their ancestors into the American West to people it with towns and cities.[98]

98. Beginning with the passage on Bryce, I have closely paraphrased or quoted directly from the concluding pages of my *Cities of the American West*.

WAGON TRAINS AT HELENA, MONTANA.—Drawn by W. M. Cary.—[See Page 98.]

Appendix: Population Data, 1850–1890 and 1970, for the Twenty Largest Western Settlements

Cities, 1850[1]		Cities, 1860		Cities, 1870	
1. San Francisco, Calif.	15,312	1. San Francisco, Calif.	56,802	1. San Francisco, Calif.	149,473
2. Sacramento, Calif.	6,820	2. Sacramento, Calif.	13,785	2. Leavenworth, Kans.	17,873
3. Placerville, Calif.	5,602[2]	3. Salt Lake City, Utah	8,236	3. Sacramento, Calif.	16,283
4. Santa Fe, N.Mex.	4,846	4. San Antonio, Tex.	8,235	4. Omaha, Nebr.	16,083
5. Marysville, Calif.	4,500[3]	5. Leavenworth, Kans.	7,429	5. Galveston, Tex.	13,818
6. Galveston, Tex.	4,177	6. Galveston, Tex.	7,307	6. Salt Lake City, Utah	12,854
7. San Antonio, Tex.	3,488	7. Houston, Tex.	4,845	7. San Antonio, Tex.	12,256
8. Nevada City, Calif.	2,675	8. Denver, Colo.	4,749	8. Oakland, Calif.	10,500
9. Houston, Tex.	2,396	9. Marysville, Calif.	4,740	9. Stockton, Calif.	10,066
10. La Cuesta, N.Mex.	2,196	10. Santa Fe, N.Mex.	4,635	10. Houston, Tex.	9,382
11. San Miguel, N.Mex.	2,008	11. San José, Calif.	4,579	11. San José, Calif.	9,089
12. Los Angeles, Calif.	1,598	12. Los Angeles, Calif.	4,385	12. Lawrence, Kans.	8,320
13. Las Vegas, N.Mex.	1,550	13. Lewiston, Calif.	4,348	13. Portland, Ore.	8,293
14. Tuckelata, N.Mex.	1,320	14. Grass Valley, Calif.	3,840	14. Atchison, Kans.	7,054
15. New Braunfels, Tex.	1,298	15. Nevada City, Calif.	3,679	15. Virginia City, Nev.	7,048
16. Pueblo de Zuni, N.Mex.	1,294	16. Stockton, Calif.	3,679	16. Nebraska City, Nebr.	6,050
17. Marshall, Tex.	1,189	17. Austin, Tex.	3,494	17. Topeka, Kans.	5,790
18. Monterey, Calif.	1,083	18. Portland, Ore.	2,874	18. Los Angeles, Calif.	5,728
19. Portland, Ore.	821	19. Brownsville, Tex.	2,734	19. Brownsville, Tex.	4,905
20. Victoria, Tex.	806	20. Bridgeport, Calif.	2,686	20. Santa Fe, N.Mex.	4,765

Cities, 1880		Cities, 1890		Urbanized Areas, 1970	
1. San Francisco, Calif.	233,959	1. San Francisco, Calif.	298,997	1. Los Angeles– Long Beach, Calif.	8,351,266
2. Denver, Colo.	35,629	2. Omaha, Nebr.	140,452	2. San Francisco– Oakland, Calif.	2,987,850
3. Oakland, Calif.	34,555	3. Denver, Colo.	106,713	3. Houston, Tex.	1,677,684
4. Omaha, Nebr.	30,518	4. Lincoln, Nebr.	55,154	4. Dallas, Tex.	1,338,684
5. Galveston, Tex.	22,248	5. Los Angeles, Calif.	50,395	5. Seattle–Everett, Wash.	1,238,107
6. Sacramento, Calif.	21,420	6. Oakland, Calif.	48,682	6. San Diego, Calif.	1,198,323
7. Salt Lake City, Utah	20,768	7. Portland, Ore.	46,385	7. Kansas City, Mo. and Kans.	1,101,787
8. San Antonio, Tex.	20,550	8. Salt Lake City, Utah	44,843	8. Denver, Colo.	1,047,311
9. Portland, Ore.	17,577	9. Seattle, Wash.	42,837	9. San José, Calif.	1,025,273
10. Leavenworth, Kans.	16,546	10. Kansas City, Kans.	38,316	10. Phoenix, Ariz.	863,357
11. Houston, Tex.	16,513	11. San Antonio, Tex.	37,673	11. Portland, Ore. and Wash.	824,926
12. Topeka, Kans.	15,452	12. Dallas, Tex.	36,067	12. San Antonio, Tex.	772,513
13. Atchison, Kans.	15,105	13. Tacoma, Wash.	36,006	13. Fort Worth, Tex.	676,944
14. Leadville, Colo.	14,820	14. Topeka, Kans.	31,007	14. Sacramento, Calif.	633,732
15. Lincoln, Nebr.	13,003	15. Galveston, Tex.	29,084	15. San Bernardino– Riverside, Calif.	583,597
16. San José, Calif.	12,567	16. Houston, Tex.	27,557	16. Oklahoma City, Okla.	579,788
17. Los Angeles, Calif.	11,183	17. Sacramento, Calif.	26,386	17. Omaha, Nebr. and Iowa	491,776
18. Austin, Tex.	11,013	18. Pueblo, Colo.	24,558	18. Salt Lake City, Utah	479,342
19. Virginia City, Nev.	10,917	19. Wichita, Kans.	23,853	19. Tulsa, Okla.	371,499
20. Dallas, Tex.	10,358	20. Fort Worth, Tex.	23,076	20. El Paso, Tex.	337,471

Source: U.S. Census, 1850, 1860, 1870, 1880, 1890, and 1970.
1. Rank order for 1850 cannot be exactly determined since enumerators did not report the population of Salt Lake City nor the populations of several California mining towns.
2. The 1850 population figure given for Placerville, Calif., is that reported for Placerville and vicinity.
3. The 1850 population figure given for Marysville, Calif., is taken from the California state census of 1852.

BIBLIOGRAPHICAL NOTE

Historical studies of the American West are vast in number and varied in content. Many of them stem from the pioneering work of Frederick Jackson Turner, although recent scholarship places less stress on his frontier hypothesis and treats the settlement of the West as a continuation of early colonization without emphasizing the distinctive features that Turner felt were so important.

1. Turner's Works and Their Critics

Turner's seminal paper of 1893, "The Significance of the Frontier in American History," first published a year later, was subsequently revised by him, and it has been frequently reprinted. The revised version and twelve of his other essays related to the subject can be found in Turner, *The Frontier in American History* (New York, 1920). The most complete treatment of Turner's hypothesis and its impact on American historians is Ray Allen Billington, *The Frontier Thesis: Valid Interpretation of American History?* (New York, 1966). Billington's treatment is generally sympathetic.

For a series of essays overwhelmingly critical of Turner's concept, see Richard Hofstadter and Seymour Lipset, eds., *Turner and the Sociology of the Frontier* (New York, 1968). Other important studies include James D. Bennett, *Frederick Jackson Turner* (Boston, 1975); Ray Allen Billington, *Frederick Jackson Turner: Historian, Scholar, Teacher* (New York, 1973); Ray Allen Billington, *The Genesis of the Frontier Thesis: A Study in Historical Creativity* (San Marino, Calif., 1971); and George Rogers Taylor, ed., *The Turner Thesis Concerning the Role of the Frontier in American History* (Boston, 1949). See also Everett E. Edwards, comp., *The Early Writings of Frederick Jackson Turner with a List of All His Works* (Madison, Wis., 1938).

Despite its importance to a later generation of historians, Turner's initial statement on the meaning of the frontier did not elicit much published comment until nearly two decades after its publication. Possibly the earliest critical analysis was Edmond S. Meany's "The Towns of the Pacific Northwest Were

Not Founded on the Fur Trade," *American Historical Association Annual Report, 1909* (Washington, D.C., 1911), pp. 165–72. Meany limited himself to the early towns of Oregon, correctly noting that there "American settlers built for themselves fresh new towns" and that "the dramatic life of the fur trade had vanished before the dawn of the real era of town building in Old Oregon."

Such fragmentary criticism of Turner's failure to place Western urbanization in its proper perspective or to recognize the rise of towns and cities as an early manifestation of frontier settlement was rarely pursued by later critics; where this was done, it was usually related to another element of the frontier hypothesis. See Stanley Elkins and Erick McKitrick, "A Meaning for Turner's Frontier: Democracy in the Old Northwest," *Political Science Quarterly* 69 (September 1954): 321–53, and (December 1954): 565–602, the first part of which is reprinted in Hofstadter and Lipset, *Turner and the Sociology of the Frontier*, pp. 120–51. The authors pointed to the "teeming numbers" of towns founded by promoters in the region and asserted that "it was unquestionably the town from which the tone of life in Ohio, Indiana, and Illinois came to be taken, rather than from the agriculture in which an undoubted majority of the population was engaged." They concluded that the development of democratic institutions on the frontier resulted more from the necessity to create political and administrative systems for municipal government than, as Turner stated, from rural farmers exercising their individualism and self-reliance gained from experience in opening up new land for agriculture.

The role of cities did receive attention by those concerned with the "safety-valve" contention of Turner, who argued that it was the opportunity to secure cheap farmland in the West that reduced discontent in the East. One scholar demonstrated that it was in the Western cities and not on the region's farms that the bulk of Easterners found their chances for new beginnings, but he, too, was unaware of the importance of city founding in the opening of the region. See Fred A. Shannon, "A Post Mortem on the Labor-Safety-Valve Theory," *Agricultural History* 19 (January 1945): 31–37.

In the mass of scholarly literature attacking, modifying, and defending Turner's concepts of the frontier and its effects on American life, city development, when discussed at all, has usually been treated as an aspect of speculation whose major thrust was directed at agricultural lands. Some of these studies are summarized or cited in Ray Allen Billington, *The American Frontier*

(Washington, D.C., 1971, and several earlier editions), a study guide published by The American Historical Association. Representative of these works is Billington's "The Origin of the Land-Speculator as a Frontier Type," *Agricultural History* 19 (October 1945): 204–12; and Paul W. Gates, "The Role of the Land Speculator in Western Development," *Pennsylvania Magazine of History and Biography* 66 (July 1942): 314–33. This is only one of Gates's many useful contributions. See also Allan G. Bogue and Margaret B. Bogue, "'Profits' and the Frontier Land Speculator," *Journal of Economic History* 17 (March 1957): 1–24.

One of Turner's early critics pointed out that it would be more accurate to state that "the picture . . . of a succession of waves of immigration is incorrect. The figure should be a flood," and that all classes of Western settlers arrived "practically simultaneously." Clarence W. Alvard, Review of Turner's *The Frontier in American History*, in *Mississippi Valley Historical Review* 7 (March 1921): 403–7. Although Billington, in his major work, *Westward Expansion: A History of the American Frontier* (New York, 1949, and later editions), retained an elaboration on Turner's analysis of a strict sequence of occupancy in which towns were the last to appear and then grew without plan, elsewhere he conceded that "at times the first-comers on a new frontier might be backwoods farmers or land speculators, at others town planters or grist millers who hoped that a village would grow up around the favorable spot they selected." Billington also pointed out that Turner had ignored altogether "the town planters or promoters who flung their dream villages into the very depth of the wilderness." *The American Frontier*, 2d ed. (1965), p. 18.

Jackson K. Putnam, in his "The Turner Thesis and the Westward Movement: A Reappraisal," *Western Historical Quarterly* 7 (October 1976): 377–404, reaffirmed many of Turner's propositions but pointed out that his "description of the frontier process suffers from at least three serious defects." One of these, according to Putnam, was Turner's notion of the strict sequence of occupancy of frontier regions. Putnam correctly observed that "the settlement process was often a headlong rush of various and competing types with the town builder especially jumping the gun in the race."

An earlier, longer, and much sharper criticism of Turner's thesis focused on this point, using St. Louis as a case study. See John Francis McDermott, "The

Frontier Re-examined," in McDermott, ed., *The Frontier Re-examined* (Urbana, Ill., 1967), pp. 1–13. McDermott concluded: "It was not the runaways from civilization skulking in the forests or the ax bearers striding forward in manly chorus, rifle in hand, bearing the light into the wilderness, but the men of capital and enterprise who opened the western country. It is from a study of their lives and works, of the towns they built and the countryside over which they operated, of the culture they brought with them, that we will come at last to a knowledge of the frontier world as it really was."

Most studies of Turner simply accepted the existence of urban communities in the West and did not inquire deeply into the circumstances of their origins or of their creation as planned communities at the very beginning of settlement. The bulk of the Turnerian literature is simply not concerned with urbanism and concentrates on the more philosophical issues involved with the impact of the frontier on the American psyche. In places the exegesis of the master's words, their textual analysis, examination of definitions, and reinterpretation of his ideas approach the theological in tone and character.

2. Histories of the West

Most of the early general histories of Westward expansion and the frontier experience, as well as many of recent vintage, ignore or fail to treat adequately the importance of towns and cities in the region, their appearance at the start of settlement, and the roles they played in the West's social, economic, and political life. See, for example, such standard works as Frederic L. Paxon, *History of the American Frontier, 1763–1893* (Boston, 1924); Billington, *Westward Expansion*; John A. Hawgood, *America's Western Frontiers: The Story of the Explorers and Settlers Who Opened up the Trans-Mississippi West* (New York, 1967); Thomas D. Clark, *Frontier America: The Story of the Westward Movement* (New York, 1969); Robert V. Hine, *The American West: An Interpretive History* (Boston, 1973); Arrell Morgan Gibson, *The West in the Life of the Nation* (Lexington, Mass., 1976); and Frederick Merk, *History of the Westward Movement* (New York, 1978).

Not all formal and serious history is conveyed by articles and books. One large museum devoted entirely to Western settlement has been visited annually by what must be many times more persons than have read all the books ever written on how the West was won. This is located at a major national park, The Jefferson National Expansion Memorial in St. Louis. Its exhibits are elaborate, impressive, and expensive, but aside from a small section showing a few mining camps it contains nothing whatsoever about Western urbanism. The leaflet distributed to visitors accurately describes what they will see: "The Museum of Westward Expansion tells the story of . . . Indians, explorers, sailors, trappers, miners, cowboys, and farmers and their families." It is, therefore, as much a museum about the myth American historians have made of the West as about the West itself.

Among the recent general books on Western settlement, two contain chapters on urban development. That in Allan G. Bogue, Thomas D. Phillips, and James E. Wright, *The West of the American People* (Itasca, Ill., 1970), is brief but discerning. It is especially valuable in pointing out the wide variety of reasons towns were established, the forces that influenced growth or decline, and the fact that while "town dwellers were but a fraction of the total population . . . their cities and their towns were the foci of economic activity and townsmen themselves were significant beyond their numbers." They also credit aggressive entrepreneurial activity in town promotion as a factor influencing differential rates of urban growth along with the more traditional explanations of advantages of particular sites or of a general location with respect to trade or transportation routes. However, although they point out the major role of townsite speculators in platting towns, they do not make explicit that towns were planned throughout the frontier by a variety of other individuals, groups, or public agencies and that these plans shaped the patterns of development for many generations.

More valuable is the longer chapter in Richard Bartlett's *The New Country* (New York, 1974), which broadly surveys the entire scope of Western urbanization and notes the appearance of towns and cities at the earliest stages of settlement. Nonetheless, even Bartlett fails to emphasize the extent to which nearly all Western cities had their origins as planned communities whose physical forms were determined in advance by individuals, corporations, railroad land agencies, colonization societies, religious groups, or territorial, state, or federal officials.

3. Collections of Readings

The same shortcomings characterize collections of documents, laws, descriptions, and other readings of Western history produced for student use in courses on the subject. A few useful selections on town founding appear in Martin Ridge and Ray Allen Billington, eds., *America's Frontier Story: A Documentary History of Westward Expansion* (New York, 1969), but they deal with minor towns and untypical cases. At least one document has been edited to omit altogether an important, revealing, and unusual passage concerned directly with urban planning in Texas under Mexican rule.

Bayard Still's *The West: Contemporary Records of America's Expansion Across the Continent, 1607–1890* (New York, 1961), also contains some material on urbanism, but he understated the point and failed to develop it when he observed in the introduction that "more omnipresent than is generally realized were the speculators, the land agents and townsite promoters, who induced and negotiated the individual acquisition of much of the West." This limited emphasis is difficult to understand when one considers his earlier perceptive observation in "Patterns of Mid-Nineteenth Century Urbanization in the Middle-West," *Mississippi Valley Historical Review* 28 (September 1941): 187–206: "On many a frontier the town builder was as conspicuous as the farmer pioneer; the western city, through the efforts of its founders to extend its economic hinterland, actually facilitated the agrarian development of the West; and the opportunities attending city growth as well as those afforded by cheap farm lands contributed to the dynamic sense of economic abundance felt by Americans of the mid-nineteenth century."

In *The Frontier Experience: Readings in the Trans-Mississippi West* (Belmont, Calif., 1963), Robert V. Hine and Edwin R. Bingham introduce their short selection of readings on Western town life with this misleading comment: "Most of the towns and cities of the West grew haphazardly by accretions of individuals, with little community planning or cohesion." The editors compound this error by stating that except for New England and a few religious or utopian settlements elsewhere, American communities were not planned. They and most other historians have yet to discover or digest the growing literature on the history of city planning in the United States demonstrating that America is a nation of planned cities, although the results were certainly not always, or even mainly, attractive or beneficial.

4. Studies of the Public Domain

The use of strategic portions of the federal public domain for urban purposes is almost entirely neglected in the many otherwise thorough studies of the U.S. public lands. See, for example, Benjamin Hibbard, *A History of Public Land Policies* (New York, 1924, rev. ed., 1939); Roy Robbins, *Our Landed Heritage* (Lincoln, Nebr., 1962); Louis Peffer, *The Closing of the Public Domain* (Palo Alto, Calif., 1951); and Vernon Carstensen, ed., *The Public Lands: Studies in the History of the Public Domain* (Madison, Wis., 1968). Only the much earlier study by Thomas C. Donaldson, *The Public Domain* (Washington, D.C., 1884), provides a list—far from complete—of the townsite claims entered under the provisions of the federal statutes.

5. Urban Histories

Of the several useful urban histories treating groups of Western towns, the earliest directly challenged the Turner frontier concept by beginning with a statement that "the towns were the spearheads of the frontier," and ending with the conclusion that "any historical view which omits this dimension of Western life tells but part of the story." This is Richard Wade's *The Urban Frontier: The Rise of Western Cities, 1790–1830* (Cambridge, Mass., 1959). While limited in time and concerned with an earlier West centering on Pittsburgh, St. Louis, Cincinnati, Louisville, and Lexington, Wade thus pushed the inquiry into new regions beyond those colonial urban frontiers so thoroughly explored by Carl Bridenbaugh in his *Cities in the Wilderness: The First Century of Urban Life in America, 1625–1742* (New York, 1938), and *Cities in Revolt: Urban Life in America, 1743–1776* (New York, 1955).

Several other studies followed the pattern pioneered by Bridenbaugh and continued by Wade. The most important are Robert R. Dykstra, *The Cattle Towns* (New York, 1968); Kenneth W. Wheeler, *To Wear a City's Crown: The Beginnings of Urban Growth in Texas, 1836–1865* (Cambridge, Mass., 1968); and Gunther Barth, *Instant Cities: Urbanization and the Rise of San Francisco and Denver* (New York, 1975), whose title fails to reveal its wider scope. Two others of lesser merit but helpful nonetheless are Robert L. Martin, *The City Moves West: Economic and Industrial Growth in Central West Texas* (Austin, 1969);

and John Alley, *City Beginnings in Oklahoma Territory* (Norman, Okla., 1939). Other urban histories focus on special categories of Western towns, such as James B. Allen, *The Company Town in the American West* (Norman, Okla., 1966); and Duane A. Smith, *Rocky Mountain Mining Camps: The Urban Frontier* (Bloomington, Ind., 1967). Not all of these works make clear that their findings offer vital evidence that could be used to test the Turnerian contention that rural and not urban life established the character of Western society. An appendix in Dykstra's book on one aspect of the Turner thesis and how the author's findings relate to it does not mention the issue of the sequence of settlement or that most Western towns were created by townsite planners.

A valuable study of the role of cities in American culture is Diana Klebanow, Franklin L. Jonas, and Ira M. Leonard, *Urban Legacy: The Story of America's Cities* (New York, 1977). The only portion devoted to the West is a brief but perceptive section on urbanization in the Great Plains and a few paragraphs on Western seaports. The authors quote Josiah Strong's 1855 observations that "the city stamps the country, instead of the country stamping the city. It is the cities and towns which will frame the state constitutions, make laws, create public opinion, establish social usages, and fix standards."

One major American urban historian, while concentrating on the various elements of life in towns and cities, apparently followed Turner in believing that urbanization occurred only after an agricultural base had been established. In her *American Cities in the Growth of the Nation* (London, 1957), Constance McLaughlin Green summarizes her conclusions on this point: "City enterprise, backed by city money, looking for new products to sell and new markets to sell to, was a force as powerful in peopling the country as the restless urge that drove the trapper perpetually on into the wilderness and the homesteader in his wake. For hard on their heels came men intent upon exploiting the new country in other ways—by marketing furs and hides, lumber, minerals, and farm produce, by speculating in real estate, by lending money and giving credit; in short, by building up the life of older cities and by founding new."

The most important volume on cities in the West related to the material in this study is Lawrence H. Larsen, *The Urban West at the End of the Frontier* (Lawrence, Kans., 1978). Using the hitherto largely overlooked, highly detailed, two-volume report on American cities in the 1880 census, Larsen demonstrates that Western cities grew with amazing speed and that, well before the supposed "closing" of the frontier in 1890, they closely resembled those elsewhere in the nation. An earlier version of his findings appeared in Lawrence H. Larsen and Robert L. Branyan, "The Development of an Urban Civilization on the Frontier of the American West," *Societas—A Review of Social History* 1 (Winter 1971): 33–50. Their final paragraph is worth noting: "City life familiar to Easterners moved west very quickly. Whether it involved transportation, fire protection, or sanitation newer cities drew on the technology of the older ones. Indeed occasionally, a western city would lead the way as San Francisco did with parks and Denver did with street lighting. By the decade of the 1880s the cities of the Great West, despite the mythology fostered by numerous pulp magazines and dime authors, simply were not frontier outposts. As the United States became a nation of cities, the physical characteristics of western urban centers differed little from their eastern counterparts."

For two surveys of the literature on Western towns that emphasize the work of urban historians, see Christopher Schnell and Patrick McLear, "Why the Cities Grew: A Historiographical Essay on Western Urban Growth, 1850–1880," *Missouri Historical Society Bulletin* 27 (April 1972): 162–77; and Bradford Luckingham, "The City in the Westward Movement—A Bibliographical Note," *Western Historical Quarterly* 5 (July 1974): 295–306. For suggestions concerning "a conceptual framework enabling us objectively to understand the process resulting in . . . [Western cities] . . . , the nature of the urbanism created and generated, and its effect upon the social, cultural, and economic well-being of the people involved," see Ronald L. F. Davis, "Western Urban Development: A Critical Analysis," in Jerome O. Steffen, ed., *The American West: New Perspectives, New Dimensions* (Norman, Okla., 1979), pp. 175–96.

6. Histories of Western Subregions and Collected Western Studies

Chapters in histories of portions of the West or in volumes presenting the work of several authors also use material related closely to the Turner thesis. Their authors generally approach urban matters, however, with a different perspective. A thorough factual exploration of urban origins in the Dakotas, Wyoming, and Montana can be found in Harold E. Briggs, *Frontiers of the Northwest: A History of the Upper Missouri Valley* (New York, 1950), pp. 347–484. Everett Dick included a valuable chapter dealing with town development in his *The Lure of the Land* (Lincoln, Nebr., 1970). Neither Dick nor Briggs, however, treats town founding, planning, and development as anything more than a result of agricultural expansion except in their descriptions of mining towns.

Earl Pomeroy, however, in his *The Pacific Slope: A History of California, Oregon, Washington, Idaho, Utah, and Nevada* (New York, 1965), suggests more strongly than Briggs and Dick that urbanization in the Far West might be worth examining as a phenomenon separate from the simultaneous or slightly later agricultural settlement of the frontier. Even more sharply focused is his fine "The Urban Frontier of the Far West," in John G. Clark, ed., *The Frontier Challenge: Responses to the Trans-Mississippi West* (Lawrence, Kans., 1971), pp. 7–29.

Mormon historians, who have written at length on almost every other aspect of their religion, have strangely neglected the wholesale town planning that represents one of the major accomplishments of the Mormons. Lowry Nelson, *The Mormon Village: A Pattern and Technique of Land Settlement* (Salt Lake City, 1952), contains much helpful information but is concerned more with the sociology of community life. The best single book-length study is Joel E. Ricks, *Forms and Methods of Early Mormon Settlement in Utah and the Surrounding Region, 1847 to 1877* (Logan, Utah, 1964). In a one-paragraph introduction, Ricks points out that Turner's description of "successive waves" of occupancy of the frontier did not fit the Mormon experience in Utah where both pioneer and permanent settlers arrived at the same time. It is unfortunate that Ricks did not draw on the rich resources of graphic material available to him to illustrate his monograph, which is otherwise amply documented.

In Milton Hunter, *Brigham Young the Colonizer* (Salt Lake City, 1940), one can find in the appendix a list of the more than 350 towns founded during Young's thirty years as head of the church in Utah, although the maps showing their locations are almost illegible. Many of the writings of Leonard Arrington, notably *Great Basin Kingdom* (Cambridge, Mass., 1958), contain valuable material on town founding, but neither he nor Hunter emphasizes how their findings and conclusions demonstrate the inadequacies of the Turner thesis as applied to Western urbanization. More recent is the exhaustive and fascinating study of Joseph Smith's last Mormon town by Robert B. Flanders, *Nauvoo: Kingdom on the Mississippi* (Urbana, Ill., 1965). But again the relationship of the Mormon urban experience to the frontier hypothesis is left unexplored.

Also useful are the contributions by two geographers: Richard H. Jackson, "The Mormon Village: Genesis and Antecedents of the City of Zion Plan," *Brigham Young University Studies* 17 (Winter 1977): 223–40; and Richard V. Francaviglia, *The Mormon Landscape: Existence, Creation, and Perception of a Unique Image in the American West* (New York, 1978). The population in 1970 of Mormon towns in Utah exceeding five hundred is given with their founding dates in Eugene E. Campbell, "Early Colonization Patterns," chap. 8 in Richard D. Poll, et al., eds., *Utah's History* (Provo, Utah, 1978), pp. 133–52.

7. Mining Camps and Towns

Virtually all of the books on the growth of mining camps and towns and their supply centers ignore Turner and the literature dealing with his concepts. Perhaps the sudden emergence of these communities offered a too obvious refutation to his explanation of how the frontier was settled, or possibly the implications of overnight urbanization escaped the authors of these works. The best single study is William S. Greever, *The Bonanza West: The Story of the Western Mining Rushes, 1849–1900* (Norman, Okla., 1963). For an excellent regional study, see also Phyllis Flanders Dorset, *The New Eldorado: The Story of Colorado's Gold and Silver Rushes* (New York, 1970). The literature on individual mining camps, on ghost towns of the mining frontier, and picture books of those in the several states where they existed is extensive, but they fail to relate these towns to the larger framework of Western urban growth or to the settlement of the frontier in its broader associations. An older study that attempted to deal with mining towns in a theoretical context, first published in 1885, can still be consulted with profit: Charles Shinn, *Mining Camps: A Study in American Frontier Government* (New York, 1948).

8. Railroad Histories

Comprehensive histories of American railroads are generally disappointing in omitting any but the briefest mention of the extensive town-founding activities of the transcontinental lines and the many other railroads that filled out the transportation network of the West. Unique in its primary emphasis on the influence of railroads on urbanization is an important but often overlooked early study: Glenn Chesney Quiett, *They Built the West: An Epic of Rails and Cities* (New York, 1934), marred by its paucity of citations to documentary sources. A few histories of individual lines provide useful details on town promotion efforts; among them are Richard C. Overton, *Burlington West: A Colonization History of the Burlington Railroad* (Cambridge, Mass., 1941); and, even better, V. V. Masterson, *The Katy Railroad and the Last Frontier* (Norman, Okla., 1952). None of these studies explicitly contradicts that portion of the Turner hypothesis asserting that towns were the last to develop in the sequence of frontier settlement, but some of them contain the necessary evidence.

9. Histories of Individual Cities

Biographies of individual cities are legion. They include scores of typical nineteenth-century "mug books," emphasizing local worthies and their alleged contributions to the prosperity and civic well-being of the community, several reasonably well-researched books with at least a few citations to sources, and some solid volumes with scholarly credentials. Among the latter there are all too few that devote more than a paragraph or two to the physical designs established by town founders and the manner in which the original patterns of streets, blocks, and open spaces were extended as population increased. Two recent studies that recognize the importance of the city as an artifact are Roger Sale, *Seattle, Past to Present* (Seattle, 1976), and Roger W. Lotchin's *San Francisco, 1846–1856: From Hamlet to City* (New York, 1974). Richard Wade's brief foreword to Lotchin's book provides for it a more theoretical framework than is offered by the author.

The modern reader searching for information on the founding of individual cities is better served by periodical literature in history and geography. He should consult two extremely fine bibliographies: Oscar O. Winther, comp., *A Classified Bibliography of the Periodical Literature of the Trans-Mississippi West, 1811–1957* (Bloomington, Ind., 1961), and (with Richard A. Van Orman) its *Supplement, (1957–1967)* (Bloomington, Ind., 1970); and the now partly dated Douglas R. McManis, comp., *Historical Geography of the United States: A Bibliography* (Ypsilanti, Mich., 1965). The most extensive bibliography focusing on Western town founding and concentrating on urban planning is in the recent volume from which the present study was drawn: John W. Reps, *Cities of the American West: A History of Frontier Urban Planning* (Princeton, 1979), pp. 747–73.

10. City Planning Histories

Only one comprehensive town planning history of the American West exists, the work cited immediately above. For the Spanish period in Texas, New Mexico, Arizona, and California—as well as the adjoining region in northern Mexico—Oakah L. Jones, Jr.'s richly informative *Los Paisanos: Spanish Settlers on the Northern Frontier of New Spain* (Norman, Okla., 1979) provides an exhaustive treatment of town planning and development under the Laws of the Indies and subsequent regulations. Its bibliographical essay is surely the most comprehensive guide to the subject yet published.

The other major published study with urban planning as its principal focus is Mel Scott's exhaustively researched and readable regional study, *The San Francisco Bay Area: A Metropolis in Perspective* (Berkeley, 1959). Unfortunately, still unpublished is Daniel Garr's "Hispanic Colonial Settlement in California: Planning and Urban Development on the Frontier: 1769–1850" (Ph.D. dissertation, Cornell University, 1972), which explores Southern California during its Hispanic period as Scott did the major towns of Northern California in the nineteenth and early twentieth centuries, although in a different way.

Urban planning of a special kind, also in Southern California, is the subject of Glenn S. Dumke's splendidly documented study of speculative towns and the effect of real estate promotion, *The Boom of the Eighties in Southern Califor-*

nia (San Marino, Calif., 1963). It should be read with Remi A. Nadeau, *City-Makers: The Men Who Transformed Los Angeles from Village to Metropolis During the First Great Boom, 1868–76* (Garden City, N.Y., 1948). Neither book pays any attention to Turner and his hypothesis, but both amply document the importance on the American frontier of townsite speculators, although in the case of Southern California the agricultural frontier was, of course, well established before the land booms of the 1870s and 1880s. For speculation in urban land as a major force in creating towns elsewhere in the West, consult the bibliographies in Winther, McManis, and Reps, cited above, although the reader should not expect to find many references that explicitly tie the material presented to the Turnerian thesis.

11. Historical Geography

By far the most important contribution by a geographer to the Turner debate is Howard J. Nelson's "Town Founding and the American Frontier," *Yearbook of the Association of Pacific Coast Geographers* 36 (Corvallis, Ore., 1974), pp. 7–23. Nelson cites the conflicting statements by Richard Wade and Ray Billington on the priority of urban or agricultural settlement. He attempted to test their validity by plotting the frontier lines for each ten-year period from 1790 to 1860, with each map showing the locations of towns with a 1970 population of fifty thousand or more that had been newly platted during the preceding ten years. Texas is omitted because of the lack of census data on density of settlement.

Nelson concludes that the Turner-Billington thesis cannot be supported. Based on his analysis he states that "the city-founding process appears to be a feature of the first wave of agricultural settlers into an area, the frontier of the 'pioneer farmers,'" rather than "later when 'equipped farmers' and specialists with capital arrived," and that "growth of towns to urban status may have been characteristic of a final 'urban frontier,' but town founding in itself was not."

Nelson, however, also rejects Wade's "notion that towns were founded as 'spearheads' holding the land for the approaching settler." It should be pointed out that 1860 is his terminal date, and that his use of decennial maps—necessary because of data limitations—can be quite misleading. In the last map of his series, for example, the towns of Kansas and Nebraska are shown somewhat to the east of the frontier line as mapped according to population density prevailing in 1860. The major towns in this area, of course, were established in 1854, with many others added during the next three years. A frontier line drawn at that time, rather than in 1860, would reveal many "vanguards" and perhaps even a "spearhead" or two. His earlier maps showing Sacramento and the first towns of Oregon suffer from the same limitation.

Everett G. Smith, Jr., in an earlier geographic analysis, relied less on census material than on studies of individual settlement dates. He correctly concludes that "town building in Oregon coincided with or preceded the breaking of the sod." See his "An Urban Interpretation of Oregon Settlement," *Yearbook of the Association of Pacific Coast Geographers* 29 (1967): 43–52.

The use of post office locations has been explored as a possible method of determining the existence of nucleated settlements in the West. Assuming that post offices are essentially urban institutions and using the dates of their establishment from federal records, two scholars have used them to trace the movement of the frontier in Montana and Kansas. See John A. Alwin, "Post Office Locations and the Historical Geographer: A Montana Example," *The Professional Geographer* 26 (May 1974): 183–86; and James R. Shortridge, "The Post Office Frontier in Kansas," *Journal of the West* 13 (July 1974): 83–97.

Maps produced by Shortridge show the settled area as indicated by the existence of post offices. They are plotted on a township basis instead of by counties, the unit used by the census to locate the frontier beyond areas with an average density of two or more persons per square mile. Moreover, Shortridge uses five-year periods rather than the decennial intervals of the census. If post offices can be regarded as a reliable guide to nucleated settlement, it is clear from Shortridge's maps that urban communities existed well beyond the frontier lines as defined by the census. Their "spearhead" or "vanguard" character is obvious, for example, if one compares the frontier line of 1860 with the townships having post offices created during the periods 1860 to 1864 or even 1855 to 1859.

For earlier contributions by historical geographers, consult the bibliography compiled by McManis and cited in Section 9 of this note. Not all geographers yet recognize the importance of town plans in their investigations. In Richard H. Jackson and Robert L. Layton, "The Mormon Village: Analysis of a Settlement Type," *The Professional Geographer* 28 (May 1976): 135–41, the authors try to identify the characteristics that set the Mormon towns apart from others of the frontier. Unaccountably, they completely ignore their most distinctive feature—the alternating lot frontage system found in so many of them and based on Joseph Smith's design of 1833.

12. Suggestions for Further Research on Western Urbanism

Material in this book and its parent volume, as well as in those cited above, offers many possibilities for additional investigation into Western town founding, planning, functions, and urban form. The best summary of work yet to be done can be found in a provocative article that raises dozens of unanswered questions: Oliver Knight, "Toward an Understanding of the Western Town," *Western Historical Quarterly* 4 (January 1973): 27–42. If the reader believes that Western urban history has already been thoroughly mined, he will quickly change his attitude when he discovers this treasure chart to the riches that remain to be found in the still underexploited mother lode of Western urban history and geography.

INDEX

ILLUSTRATION CREDITS

Note: Numbers given in the illustration credits are figure numbers rather than page numbers.

American Antiquarian Society: 51

Amon Carter Museum of Western Art: 13, 22, 41, 42, 66, 86, 87

Bancroft Library, University of California, Berkeley: 11, 30, 61, 68, 80, 83

Barker Texas History Center Archives, University of Texas, Austin: 24

The British Library: 2, 4

Bureau of Land Management: 38, 45

California Historical Society: 70

California State Archives: 12, 77

California State Library: 8, 65

Church of Jesus Christ of Latter-Day Saints: 88, 93

Colorado State Historical Society: 37, 43

Cornell University, Olin Library: 17, 44, 96

Dallas County Clerk, Dallas, Texas: 21

Fresno County Recorder of Deeds, Fresno, California: 82

Houston, Texas Public Library: 18

The Huntington Library: 10

Junipero Serra Museum: 76

Kansas State Historical Society: 53

King County Recorder of Deeds, Seattle, Washington: 32

Library Association of Portland, Oregon: 27, 28

Library of Congress, Geography and Map Division: 16, 19, 23, 31, 33, 40, 48, 50, 52, 58, 60, 62, 64, 67, 69, 73, 75, 78, 79, 81, 84, 95, 98

Library of Congress, Prints and Photographs Division: 54

Los Angeles County Museum of Natural History: 71

Marion County Recorder of Deeds, Salem, Oregon: 26

Nebraska State Historical Society: 46, 59

Nevada State Historical Society: 36, 57

New York Public Library: 35, 99

The Oakland Museum: 9

Oregon Historical Society: 29

John W. Reps: 1, 7, 14, 15, 74, 89, 92, 94

The Rosenberg Library: 20

Salt Lake County Recorder of Deeds, Salt Lake City, Utah: 90

San Bernardino County Recorder of Deeds, San Bernardino, California: 91

Security Pacific National Bank, Los Angeles, California: 6

Tacoma, Washington, Public Library: 85

Title Insurance and Trust Company, San Diego, California: 72

University of California Press, Berkeley: 3

U.S. National Archives and Record Service, Cartographic and Architectural Division: 25, 39, 47, 49, 55, 63, 97, 100

Walla Walla County Recorder of Deeds, Walla Walla, Washington: 34

The Witte Museum: 5

Wyoming State Archives and Historical Department: 56